"In China, we have a saying that we commonly apply to our inner cultivation practice: ZhanZuoXingWoBuLiZheGe 站坐行臥不離這個, which means never depart from 'This' whenever you are standing, sitting, walking, or reclining. What is 'This' and how do we stay with 'This'? In Cain Carroll's *The Four Dignities*, you will find the answers!"

—*Master Zhongxian Wu, lifelong Daoist practitioner and author of 12 books (5 in Chinese) on Chinese wisdom traditions*

"Cain Carroll has produced a must-have book that is essential reading for any self-respecting person on the path of self-cultivation. A wonderful collection of wisdom from diverse traditions that serves to illuminate the simple universal truths at their heart. This book needs to be with you standing, walking, sitting, or lying down."

—*Gordon Faulkner, Principal Instructor, Chanquanshu School of Daoist Arts and author of* Managing Stress with Qigong

"The Four Dignities form the basis of all Eastern wisdom traditions and this book provides a comprehensive overview of the nature of sitting, standing, walking, and lying down in the internal arts. As well as this are a host of other useful sections on the nature of mind/consciousness and the path of internal cultivation. This is a great book for those engaged in any form of spiritual training."

—*Damo Mitchell, author of* Daoist Nei Gong *and* Heavenly Streams *by the same author*

Mudras of India
A Comprehensive Guide to the Hand
Gestures of Yoga and Indian Dance
Cain Carroll and Revital Carroll
Foreword by Dr. David Frawley
ISBN 978 1 84819 084 9 (hardback)
ISBN 978 1 84819 109 9 (paperback)
eISBN 978 0 85701 067 4

Mudras of Yoga
72 Hand Gestures for Healing and Spiritual Growth
Cain Carroll
With Revital Carroll
Card Set
ISBN 978 1 84819 176 1
eISBN 978 0 85701 143 5

Mudras of Indian Dance
52 Hand Gestures for Artistic Expression
Revital Carroll
With Cain Carroll
Card Set
ISBN 978 1 84819 175 4
eISBN 978 0 85701 142 8

THE FOUR DIGNITIES

The Spiritual Practice of Walking,
Standing, Sitting, and Lying Down

CAIN CARROLL

SINGING
DRAGON
LONDON AND PHILADELPHIA

First published in 2015
by Singing Dragon
an imprint of Jessica Kingsley Publishers
73 Collier Street
London N1 9BE, UK
and
400 Market Street, Suite 400
Philadelphia, PA 19106, USA

www.singingdragon.com

Library of Congress Cataloging in Publication Data
Carroll, Cain, author.
  The four dignities : the spiritual practice of walking,
standing, sitting, and lying down / Cain Carroll.
    pages cm
  Includes bibliographical references and index.
  ISBN 978-1-84819-216-4 (alk. paper)
  1. Spiritual life. 2. Posture. I. Title.
  BL624.C3477 2014
  204'.46--dc23
                              2014015064

British Library Cataloguing in Publication Data
A CIP catalogue record for this book is available from the British Library

ISBN 978 1 84819 216 4
eISBN 978 0 85701 166 4

Printed and bound in Great Britain

To Susan Carroll (1946–2004),
my mother, dear friend, and first meditation teacher

ACKNOWLEDGMENTS

I am eternally grateful to my wife, Revital Carroll, for her support, patience, and editorial suggestions. To all of my teachers who have graciously guided me along the Way: Master Zhongxian Wu, Liu Ming, Drupon Khenpo Lodro Namgyal, Liu Shan, Ramkohea, Banambar Baba, Baba Hari Das, Sat Jivan Singh, Adi Singh, Sun Yogi Umashankar, Yogi Das, Dr. Yogi Vikeshanand, Sensei Mike Noriega, and Gerow Reece. Special thanks to Master Zhongxian Wu for his contribution and help with Chinese phrases; to Kazuaki Tanahashi for his support in researching Buddhist references to the Four Dignities; and Laraine Herring for her friendship and generosity with editorial suggestions. To all of my students for keeping up with the practice and requesting I write this book, and to all the people at Singing Dragon who worked to bring it to life…thank you.

CONTENTS

INTRODUCTION

"'Sitting in meditation' does not simply mean to sit with the body erect and the eyes closed. This is superficial sitting. To sit authentically, you must maintain a heart-mind like Mount Tai, remaining unmovable and unshakable throughout the entire day. Maintain this practice whether standing, walking, sitting, or lying down, whether in movement or stillness."

Chongyang Shiwu Lun[1]

Through centuries of exploration and experimentation, adepts, mystics, and yogis have made priceless discoveries about the human condition. Many of their findings centered on understanding the causes of suffering and how to alleviate them. They understood that the majority of our life happens while walking, standing, sitting, and lying down. They realized that these four positions serve as a type of blueprint from which all our experiences are constructed. Whatever we do, feel, or think is affected by our posture, breathing, and awareness.

Since the variations of thought, speech, and action are almost limitless, ancient adepts proposed the idea that the four bodily positions serve as the basis for self-cultivation. The art of self-cultivation, they explained, is like growing rice. Through clear understanding of natural law, and cooperation with environmental forces, a farmer cultivates the land and brings forth the potential crop. The farmer cannot claim to have made the rice grow by his personal efforts alone. Sun, wind, rain, soil, and so many other factors are also at play. The potential exists in the land, yet the rice fields would not flourish without the farmer's attendance. The future rice plant is contained in a seed. To be actualized, however, a seed requires the proper conditions and treatment. Farming is a prime example of cooperation and timing.

So it is with self-cultivation. For a person interested in spiritual practice, body and mind become the field of cultivation. Original Nature is the seed, as well as the fruit. The seed is necessary to grow the fruit, and the fruit is the source of the seed. Who can say which came first? Original Nature is not found outside of body and mind. It is not found inside either. Yet body and mind must be cultivated to actualize the full potential of Original Nature.

In other words, through self-cultivation we can understand, and therefore eliminate, the causes of suffering. When ignorance ceases, basic joy bubbles up undisturbed. This idea is central to the teachings of three of the world's most prominent traditions of self-cultivation: Buddhism, Daoism, and Yoga.

The term "four dignities" is a translation of ideas found in Sanskrit, Pali, Chinese, and Japanese writings. Buddhist texts use the terms "four bodily carriages" or "four dignities." In Japanese, the term *shi gi* (四 儀) is used, meaning the "four bodily presences" or "four noble rites." The *Abhidharmakosa*[2] refers to these as the "four awesome presences" or the "four dignified rituals." Traditional Daoist lineages use the term *Si Wei Yi* (四威儀), meaning "four special actions." Daoists developed countless ways of using these special actions to improve health and nourish the spirit. The Chinese sage Ma Yu[3] writes, "You should keep your heart-mind stable for a long time. Whether walking, standing, sitting or lying down, follow the Dao." His statement summarizes the quintessence of spiritual development.

Walking, standing, sitting, and lying down are straightforward. Yet keeping the heart-mind stable during these four, as Ma Yu implores, is not as easy as it sounds. Anyone who has practiced meditation knows this all too well. Again, let us draw upon the wisdom of the ancients for further support. *Qing Jing* (清 静) is another Chinese phrase used in Daoist traditions to denote the state of clarity and calm. *Qing* means "clear," "complete," or "pure." Think of a still alpine lake. *Jing* means "quiet," "stable," or "still." Think of a remote mountain peak. *Qing Jing* implies that things are fundamentally complete and at ease.

The central point here is to remain in the *Qing Jing* state all the time. The fruit of spiritual practice manifests spontaneously when we learn to relax into natural perfection. To this end, the body and mind do not need to be rigidly controlled.

A similar approach is found in the teachings of the Japanese philosopher and master agriculturist, Masanobu Fukuoka.[4] For more than 65 years, Mr. Fukuoka taught his unique methods of sustainability and natural farming. The foundation of his technique is that to grow the best-quality crops, and ensure the long-term health of the soil, the land needs to be gently nurtured, not controlled. He taught mindfulness, patience, and collaboration with nature. Without the use of chemicals, fertilizers, weeding, or standard seeding practices, his yields matched or exceeded those of conventional farmers. His secrets? Clarity. Calm. Cooperation.

Just as the possibility of flourishing rice exists in the land, the *Qing Jing* state is native to human beings. In both cases, cultivation is the activating force. Among the myriad techniques of self-cultivation, there is one that emerges as central within the great spiritual traditions of the world. Meditation. Time-tested and perfected over countless generations, meditation is one of the most straightforward ways of realizing the full potential of body, mind, and spirit.

There are many conflicting ideas about what meditation is. Western culture has adopted meditation as another form of self-improvement. The cultural assumption is that meditation is about stilling the mind or entering altered states of consciousness. There is a common belief that the goal of meditation is to get rid of thoughts, kill the ego, or enter an otherworldly blissful trance. Such ideas are erroneous and misleading. They expose a worldview based in the cosmology of insufficiency. There is a fundamental assumption—primarily informed by the Judeo-Christian notion of original sin and subsequent need for salvation—that something is innately wrong with us. Theism postulates God and his ordained instruments as the answer to the supposed problem. But what if no such problem exists to begin with?

Popular understanding of meditation often removes the orthodox notion of God and religion from the equation, but fails to investigate the insidious assumption that one is in need of saving. In the core teachings of spiritual traditions where meditation is foremost, no such idea arises. In fact, Buddhism, Daoism, and Vedanta postulate the exact opposite: that everything is just fine. All things are faultless from the beginning.

The central teaching proposes that it is through mental projection and error of perception that we find flaw with the world and ourselves. Ignorance is the root cause of suffering. A verse from the Pali Canon reads, "The heart's nature is intrinsically radiant, defilements are only visitors."[5]

Meditation, then, is not a tool for fixing what is wrong or attaining what is absent. It is a way of directly realizing the truth, of savoring reality as-it-is. Meditation is not something esoteric. It is not an Asian aesthetic hinting at transcendence. It has very little to do with stone Buddha statues and lotus flowers. Plain and simple: meditation is an immediate relationship with what is right in front of you. Uncolored by culture, religion, or politics, true meditation exists only in the context of your direct experience.

What is Dignity?

The word dignity originates from the Latin *dignus*, meaning "worthy." It later became associated with notions of royalty and position of privilege in religion or politics. A dignitary is a person of high rank or elevated status. Dignity became something that not just anyone was thought to possess. Many people conceived of dignity as something one had to be born into, transferred from royal parents to noble heir. During the Age of Enlightenment in Europe, such definitions of dignity were challenged. Central to the Enlightenment movement was the notion that each individual possessed personal freedom and intrinsic value. It was postulated that every person was entitled to be treated with respect and dignity.

Such ideas were strongly opposed by the Church and aristocracy, whose power and control was threatened by the prospect of a liberated society. Today, the concept of dignity is colored by its varied past. Many people still associate dignity with high office or position of importance, the domain of kings and queens. However, for the purposes of this book and the endeavor of spiritual development, dignity boils down to self-honesty and self-respect. In short, being true to one's nature. In a sense, as the thinkers of the Enlightenment era proposed, dignity is native to all living beings. It is not something reserved for those of elevated station, but contained in the very fabric of all living things. It is not so much an aesthetic quality, but an inward alignment with the truth of one's heart and humanity.

This brings us back around to writings in Chinese and Sanskrit that predate the Enlightenment era by more than 1500 years. Central to Daoist thinking is the notion of *ziran* (Chinese "so-of-itself"). This is the idea that things arise of their own intrinsic nature, and that each moment or thing is complete unto itself. The word *ziran* shows up numerous times in the *Dao De Jing*. A verse from Chapter 51 reads:

> *All things arise from Dao,*
> *They are nourished by Virtue.*
> *They are formed from matter.*
> *They are shaped by environment.*
> *Thus the ten thousand things all respect Dao and honor Virtue.*
> *Respect of Dao and honor of Virtue are not demanded,*
> *But they are in the nature of things.*

Essential to the verse is the fact that respect for Dao and Virtue is not demanded, but is seen as "in the nature of things." In terms of self-cultivation, naturalness and basic goodness are the foundations of dignity. These are not granted from outside by another person or acquired by one's personal efforts. Either of these would imply that dignity is absent until gained. Like heat and fire, dignity and humanity are co-arising.

In the context of Buddhism, especially Japanese Zen, the concept of *tathatā* holds vital importance. *Tathatā* is a Sanskrit word meaning "suchness" or "thusness." Similar to *ziran*, the notion of *tathatā* connotes direct contact with the true nature of things. The purpose of study, meditation, and self-cultivation is to drop away conditioned ways of being and remain in constant harmony with reality as-it-is. The historical figure Gautama Buddha referred to himself as *Tathāgata* ("one who has realized suchness"). He did not claim to have attained a transcendent state, become a god, or to have achieved anything whatsoever. He only declared to be awake, fully conscious of the entirety of his own being. After his awakening, Gautama Buddha traveled throughout Asia and taught for 45 years. At the core of his approach was the importance of realizing *tathatā*. He taught that truth could only be realized through one's own direct experience. His two most important methods: meditation and self-reflection.

The Four Dignities is a practice of meditation in four positions. It is a practice of tending to the naked flesh of our immediate experience. It is a direct approach to touch the heart of our humanity and uncover the jewel of self-existing dignity. Such a practice is open to all who would dare embrace the totality of their own situation. It calls to those who feel the inner yearning, to those who have heard the silent roar of their own spirit and can no longer postpone its attendance. The Four Dignities is for those who yet long to penetrate the true heart of spiritual awakening.

The door is wide open. There are no prerequisites. No secret teachings. No initiation. No levels of attainment. No faith required. Each of us starts precisely where we are with self-honesty and commitment to investigate our immediate condition. Within the circumstances of our everyday life, we discover direct access to innate wisdom. We come to understand the suchness of things. Through the cultivation of ordinary awareness, natural posture, and unencumbered breathing, we uncover a hidden sanctuary of tranquility and vitality that is ever-present and always accessible.

The practice of the Four Dignities is both somatic and contemplative. We could boil the method down to two essential skills: feeling and reflecting. Through feeling and observing, we come to understand how reality functions. We see clearly how suffering is self-made. We see how affliction ensues when our conduct is in disharmony with natural law. The *Zhuangzi*[6] puts it quite poignantly: "When you argue with reality, you lose." Through daily practice, we learn how to flow along with the way things flow along.

> "Daily practice involves refining qi when residing in quiet places and refining spirit when residing in noisy places. Walking, standing, sitting and lying down *are* the Dao."
>
> *Hao Datong*[7]

Using This Book

I have divided the book into three main sections: View, Method, and Fruition. The chapters in the View section establish the philosophical basis for the Method. Our ideas about our own body and mind have an enormous impact on how we go about practicing. For example, if you approach meditation as a remedy for your problems, you will likely be let down with the results. Yet, if you use View to challenge the notion that your problems are problems, you might find that meditation exposes you to be fundamentally problem-free.

Method is the nuts and bolts of the Four Dignities. The chapters in the Method section present the meditative practices of walking, standing, sitting, and lying down. The final chapter of the section details the complete Four Dignities practice, including practical considerations such as timing, location, and use of props.

Fruition is the result of View and Method interacting. In this last section, we look at the effects of our practice. We investigate what happens from what we do. View, Method, and Fruition are a circle, not a line. From Fruition, we return and reinvestigate View. With a fresh perspective on View, we re-enter Method. The circle goes round and round. Following the circle, we expose potential pitfalls and obstacles on the path. View, Method, and Fruition support and counterbalance one another, like spokes on a wheel.

Where Words Trail Off

This entire book is about something that cannot be properly expressed in words. The whole enterprise of ink, paper, and glue fails miserably at representing the true nature of things. Nevertheless, here we are. I wrote a book. And you're reading it. As the Indian sage Ramana Maharshi said, "Once your head goes in the tiger's mouth, there is no going back."

What value can we glean from this, then? For both of us, it's the same. A little more interest in direct experience of what cannot be named. A glimmer of clarity in realizing what we actually are. A bolstered sense of confidence in the inner process of self-cultivation.

Words are like fingers pointing at a cool clear lake. The water does look lovely. Let us not stay on the shore like spectators, but dive in and know freshness for ourselves. In terms of meditation, it all comes down to one simple act repeated over and over.

Practice.

Part I

VIEW

"Practice should be seven parts study of one's nature, three parts exercise of one's body."

Qiu Chuji[8]

View is the philosophical backbone of spiritual practice. With a clear understanding of View, the physical practice of the Four Dignities (Method) will yield spontaneously beneficial results (Fruition). Without a firm understanding of View, the methods employed by any spiritual practice will serve mostly to strengthen and solidify our unchecked assumptions. If our assumptions are not in accord with reality as-it-is—and usually they are not—our practice will serve to exacerbate confusion and tighten the knot of discontentment.

In this section, we dive into the practice of contemplation. With a spirit of curiosity and sincere interest, we ask some important questions. What is a human being? What are the natural laws that govern the world we live in? What is it that puts the mind at ease? What brings joy to the heart?

We look at fundamental concepts about the nature of body, mind, spirit, and Vital Force. We investigate some of the underlying perspectives that inform the world's greatest meditative traditions. By employing the process of reflection, we gain insight into how to gracefully and effectively apply traditional wisdom within the context of our daily lives.

❦ Chapter 1 ❧

THE ART OF CONTEMPLATION

"Intense and methodical investigation into one's mind is Yoga."

Nisargadatta Maharaj

The way we conceptualize ourselves and the world largely affects how we go about doing things. Whether we are conscious of it or not, we hold a particular mental outlook—a view. A view is a set of beliefs about how we think the world works. It is a cosmology. A mythology. Much of this view is formulated in childhood by the dominant assumptions of our culture. Many of the core notions that make up our culture's worldview are established by religion, politics, and advertising. Each of these has its own agenda.

As we mature, we adopt certain beliefs based on what we deem advantageous. Maybe you are an optimist. A realist. A believer. A skeptic. A mystic. Maybe you have adopted science as your chosen mythology. Whatever the case may be, like a fish in water, your view is the medium you swim in. It's easy to forget that you have a view. If you do not check frequently, you will only operate within the framework of your view. Seems harmless.

Yet, if certain aspects of this view are not representative of reality as-it-is, you will find yourself feeling claustrophobic, uncomfortable in your own skin. No matter what you do—how much success or fun you have—there is a nagging sense of unrest. It doesn't matter how much others love and respect you, genuine fulfillment somehow seems to elude you. Even though you do everything "right," secretly inside yourself there is still a sense that something is missing.

The cause of this predicament does not lie with you or the world. Both are perfectly imperfect. The glitch is in the view. We do not taste true satisfaction until we go beyond the veil of our own concepts. We are not free until we cease to be defined by what we believe.

The art of self-reflection is the central endeavor of spiritual cultivation. It includes three main aspects: exposure, contemplation, and embodiment. Exposure means making contact with ideas that spark the process of self-reflection. Exposure can happen in many ways: reading books, listening to lectures, making a connection with a teacher, observing nature, and so on. Exposure is exciting and fresh. The inception of new possibilities usually is. Yet every honeymoon period wanes with time. Although exposure is absolutely necessary, it only reaches skin deep. The genuine value of exposure is that it ignites contemplation.

It takes courage and perseverance to touch the depths of anything, especially the human heart. The movement from exposure to contemplation is no exception. We can easily get caught in the trap of reading stacks of spiritual books, attending endless seminars, and otherwise accumulating a head-full of theoretical knowledge. Getting stuck in the exposure phase is like never leaving the buffet line. We overeat and then suffer from spiritual indigestion. At some point, we must stop and digest what we have already consumed. Digestion is less exciting than consumption; however, this is how value is extracted and assimilated.

Contemplation, in its early stages, is the ability to entertain an idea without accepting or rejecting it. It is something akin to holding a baby bird in your palm. With great interest and care, you begin to observe closely. The purpose of contemplation is to see things in a fresh way. Premature acceptance of exciting ideas closes the hand too forcefully, crushing the bird. Premature rejection of confronting concepts pushes new possibility away; the bird gets dropped. The first lesson we must learn in the art of contemplation is to calm down. We have to take ideas in fully, digest them slowly. There is no rush. We do not have to accept or reject. We do not have to label "good" or "bad." There is another option beyond the duality of choosing *this* or *that*. We can simply remain open.

The process of contemplation entails closely observing our own beliefs. The objective is not to acquire a host of new ideas per se, but to find out if the ones we hold dear have any relationship with reality. One of my teachers said it nicely: "Losing ignorance is much better than gaining any wisdom."[9] One of the benefits of properly conducted contemplation is that it exposes our own confusion. Contemplation shines the lamp of awareness into the dark rooms of our belief systems. Light can only expose our ignorance; it's up to us to toss out assumptions and beliefs that are not representative of reality as-it-is.

Exposing Assumptions

The first step in contemplating View is to point out the presence of assumptions and understand how they function. Assumptions are like eyeglasses; we usually look through them, not at them. When wearing glasses, we typically don't notice the lenses unless they are dirty. When we look at objects seen through the lenses, we assume the lenses are neutral and correct, and therefore afford an accurate view of the world we observe. After a short time of putting on new glasses, we forget they're even there.

So it is with our fundamental assumptions. Most assumptions operate behind our conscious thought and action. We've been wearing them for decades. Assumptions are clusters of ideas about the world and ourselves. We piece these together to form a conceptual operating system. Much of the content of this system was not consciously selected, but unconsciously taken on as a means of fitting in, or surviving difficult circumstances. Many of our most foundational assumptions get established before our brain is fully developed. Even after the faculties of cognitive discernment are well established, the storehouse of assumptions can remain unexamined. Over time, we build a vast repertoire of knowledge on top of our assumptions. It comes to function as our personal cosmology. The particular way we see the world is our View.

Our View has an enormous impact on the way we move, breathe, and act. There is a classic example used in Vedic philosophy that illuminates this point: A farmer returns to his home after a long day in the fields. Upon entering a dark room, he sees a snake coiled in the corner. He jumps back in fear, heart racing, and lights a lamp. As light fills the room, the man realizes the snake is actually a coiled rope. He sighs in relief. Immediately, his fear is gone. The body, however, continues to tremble for a while as stress hormones make their way through his bloodstream. This affects his posture, heart rate, breathing, and many other physiological and psychological functions. His mental and physical reactions were real. Even though, in reality, there was no snake and no threat.

Our perceptions and projections are kicking up dust all the time. Many of our worries and problems are simply snakes in the rope. Ignorance causes us to think, speak, and act in disaccord with the way things actually are. Most of our suffering arises from misperception. Misperception results from seeing the world through clouded assumptions.

The trouble is, our presumptions don't particularly like to be exposed. Assumptions, like ignorance, function best in the dark. When we begin to shine the light of awareness on our assumptions, they get a little uncomfortable. As beliefs get challenged, feelings of irritation or defensiveness can easily arise. This is usually an indication that a particular belief is concealing a more sensitive issue. Usually, it's the fact that we feel confused about more things than we care to admit. Our façade has been breached. We don't have answers to life's big questions. We're not sure who we are. We have feelings, sensations, and experiences that we don't fully understand. Beliefs and assumptions offer temporary relief. We lose ourselves in them. Like an anesthesia, they buffer the sting of immediate contact with the imperfect reality of our personal situation.

One of our culture's core assumptions is that life has to make sense. Society values knowing. We give precedence to people who know. We make a big fuss over faith, conviction, and belief. People with strong convictions seem to transcend the humbling dilemma of non-knowing. They are confident and magnetic. Charismatic. We like that. It's exciting. Maybe they know something we don't. Our cultural presumption is that if we can just get rid of uncertainty and feel solid in ourselves, we will finally be comfortable and happy.

It doesn't happen like that.

What is a Human Being?

It's easy to blow off the question. In the spirit of contemplation, however, let's not assume we have a grasp of the obvious. With contemplation, it's easy to jump to conclusions, to make sweeping statements. "Oh, I know what a human being is. I am one." Actually, it's a fascinating thing to investigate. Let's go for freshness here.

We have a strong tendency to identify with our body, intellect, emotions, personality, and possessions. We hold an underlying assumption that a human being is a clearly defined entity. A noun. We assume, as individuals, that we have a separate and distinct existence, an abiding self. I am me. You are you. It seems as if we have enduring solitary existences.

This feeling of I-am-ness is called *ahamkara* in Sanskrit. *Ahamkara* literally means "I-maker," and is sometimes more loosely translated as "ego." However, *ahamkara* is not an actual thing, but a set of conditions that together create the mirage-like appearance of a separate self. With *ahamkara* operative, the entire personal conundrum unfolds.

A similar phenomenon happens on a hot day in the desert. When conditions are just right, something quite peculiar occurs. The interplay of air density, light waves, and angle of view creates the appearance of a body of water. As you move closer to the water, it moves away. The more aggressively you chase it, the faster it vanishes. A mirage.

We are comparable. It is not so easy to pin down a concrete thing called a human being. Being human is about relatedness. A human being is not a thing, but a set of interrelated conditions. Like an ocean. There is salt, water, fish, coral, plankton, and countless other parts. Only when all of these come together do we call it an ocean.

For one person to live, innumerable factors have to come together and harmoniously relate. For example, if we stop breathing, the body dies within minutes. If we don't drink, the body dies within weeks. If we don't eat and excrete, the body will die in a matter of months. It appears as if the body is solid and enduring, a vessel we put food and drink into. However, in reality, the body is made of food and drink and breath. The human being is not a self-contained entity. We are a form that appears only under the right combination of conditions.

On the mundane level, all of this is quite obvious. We know we have to breathe, drink, and eat to live. Yet a deeper insight is available when we really understand the implications. Without relatedness, we have no existence. We can't even digest lunch without the cooperation of billions of beneficial bacteria living in our gut. Breathing is of no avail unless photosynthesizing plants, trees, and ocean-dwelling phytoplankton give off oxygen. Our existence may have more to do with what is outside our skin than what is inside. So, let's ask again: what is a human being?

Strictly speaking, there is no such thing as a human being. It is an expression of convention, a concept. To be able to talk about things, we have to give them name and form (Sanskrit *nama rupa*). Yet these names and forms are relative; they have meaning only in the realm of mental construct.

In reality, there is being. There is inter-being. We can say that human beings, like all phenomena, arise through the interaction of innumerable causes. They stick around for a while, and then fall apart. We give name and form to things as a way of understanding and talking about the world we live in. This stems from a uniquely human need to find and express meaning. We formulate beliefs that reinforce our personal understanding. Following patterns and synchronicities, we easily jump from observing relatedness to believing we've understood causation. Taking great liberties, we explain to ourselves, and each other, how and why things happen. We establish truths, and then believe them to be immutable. We do this through stories, mythology, science, and religion. Each phase of history has its delivery system *du jour*. Yet, at best, language and concepts represent a relative version of reality. This is only half of the picture.

Natural Law

There are three undeniable laws that govern the way of all things: constancy, change, and interdependence. Change is the quality of movement. Alternation. Things never stay the same. Everything is becoming something else. Transformation. The body is always changing. Thoughts are always changing. Emotions are always changing. Physical sensations, always changing. Likes, dislikes, dreams, aspirations, intuitions—all are constantly changing. The river of change is unstoppable. Not a single thing endures. Everything is impermanent.

I'm sure this is not the first time you have thought about the law of change. It's easy to understand philosophically. The mind says, "Yeah, yeah, I get it. Now what?" Yet, when we look closely at our own conduct, it is obvious we do not get it. Despite knowing full well that nothing endures, we still secretly want to feel good all the time. We think there is something wrong when we have unpleasant experiences or things don't go our way. We try to fix ourselves, the world, and everybody else. We say it must be karma, or maybe Mercury has gone retrograde. We try to figure out how and why things went wrong. We want to be young, sexy, and smart forever. Our conscious mind would not admit any of this in public. It's too absurd. It would break our disguise. Nevertheless, such desires are operative on the level of our base assumptions. We get a clear glimpse of our underlying View when we *don't* get what we want.

Nobody perfectly understands how or why the law of change works. Science has its theories. Religion postulates a god whose will is the driving force. Astrology has it explanation. The *Yijing* paints a picture. All are valid and interesting. Yet, in terms of spiritual awakening, it is not particularly relevant to understand how the law of change affects your personal story. It is essential to see how acting in contradiction to the law of change causes your own turmoil. To this end, it is helpful to investigate your relationship with change. When we pay attention to the changing dynamics within our own experience, we have the possibility of insight into universal principle. This insight is one of the most direct pathways to awakening.

On the one hand, constancy is the complementary opposite of change. The reason we can notice change is because there is a continuous background that is unchanging. Openness. Constancy is the backdrop upon which change happens—like the silver screen behind a motion picture. In terms of visual observation, we call it space. While reading, you notice the printing on the page and give little notice to the paper behind the words. In a room, you notice what stands out. Try it. Look around the location you are in right now. What is the most plentiful thing you see? Space.

Between and around every object is space. Between your eyes and this page, space. Can you see it?

In terms of listening, constancy is silence. The reason we can hear musical notes is because of the silence between them. In fact, silence is always there. It is a continuous medium within which sound resonates. Like space, silence doesn't stand out unless you notice it. Can you hear the silence?

In terms of thoughts, constancy is awareness. Are you aware that you are thinking right now? At first glance, thoughts appear as a continuous stream. When we observe more closely, we find that thoughts are similar to musical notes. Between each thought is a gap. Like objects in a room, thoughts stand out because of the space between them. Just as silence is continuous behind sounds, awareness is constant behind and between thoughts. In the art of contemplation, we look at what is there and what is not there. Part of the practice is to notice the unchanging dimension behind all phenomena.

And yet constancy has two sides. On the other hand, the law of constancy refers back to the law of change. It says that change is the only constant. If that is the case, what appears to be unchanging must also change. Our dualistic mind, with its love for tidy boxes, does not like this idea at all. It threatens intellectual certainty. It rocks the boat. Change and constancy are supposed to be opposites. But it's not that cut and dried.

Observable things have shape, size, duration, texture, or some definable quality that stands out. These can be thoughts, sensations, emotions, plants, people, planets, galaxies. We can use the word Form to describe anything that has distinctive qualities. If we are uncertain whether something meets this description, we ask four questions to clarify: Is it observable? Does it have a beginning? Does it change? Does it have an end? A yes answer to one question automatically confirms the other three.

To exercise our contemplation muscles, let us try a couple of examples. Desire. Let's say you really want to eat ice cream. Can you observe the desire? Of course. Did the desire have a beginning, or is it a continuous unwavering force? Clearly it is something that arises from time to time. Does the desire change? Definitely; the intensity and duration are always different. Does it end? Yes. Other desires arise to take its place. And, by definition, if something begins, it must also end.

Let's look at something with a much larger scope. The Sun. Can you observe it? Obviously. Does it have a beginning? Yes; according to science, our Sun is about 5 billion years old. Does it change? Yes, it is about 300 degrees hotter and about 6 percent larger in diameter than when it was first born. Does it have an end? Yes, the lifetime of the Sun is estimated at about 7.5 billion years.[10]

Form is anything that is observable, changing, and temporary. These parameters apply regardless of size, scope, duration, or subtlety. Now for the interesting part: Form only appears in conjunction with its partner, Emptiness. Emptiness is that which has no shape, no size, no duration, no definable characteristics whatsoever. In this context, empty does not mean the opposite of full. Emptiness is not a vacuum. It is vital. It means indistinguishable, non-preferential. We could use Openness as a synonym.

It would seem that Form and Emptiness are polar opposites, like spirit and matter, Republican and Democrat. Yet the law of continuity says that opposites are actually one continuum. This is obvious in politics, but a little less clear in other fields. Think of a magnet with two poles. Positive and negative are distinct, although part of the same magnet. If you cut the magnet in two, both pieces will have positive and negative poles. The law of change says that everything is becoming something else. This applies to non-things as well. Opposites turn into each other.

When you eat a carrot, you kill it. The carrot breaks down in your body and its elemental parts are used to build new cells. Death becomes life. After your body expires, it will start to decompose. Life becomes death. Maybe a bunch of carrots will grow out of the soil that was once your body. Death becomes life. This is not morbid. It is the very mechanism of life's self-renewing circle. When we apply the laws of continuity and change to Emptiness and Form, we discover a singular unbroken reality with two expressions. The life matrix is "more than one, less than two," as Indian Bhakti Yogis are fond of saying. Like a magnet with two poles, Form and Emptiness are one body. Perhaps the *Heart Sutra*[11] explains it best:

> Form is not different from Emptiness, Emptiness is not
>   different from Form;
> Form is exactly Emptiness, Emptiness is exactly Form.
> Form, sensation, perception, mindful conduct, and
>   consciousness
> are all of them just like this.

The law of Interdependence states that nothing has singular individuated existence. No single thing exists by itself. All things are composite, made of multiple parts. Even the parts are made of parts. These are the basic elemental building blocks of all things. The building blocks themselves are composite and continuously changing. Think of water. All living things contain it. The human body is about 60 percent water. We don't own that water. The water doesn't stay in the body as it would in a balloon. New water moves in and old water moves out, constantly. We know that water itself is not a singular thing. It is made of molecules. Molecules are not singular things either. They are made of atoms: in the case of water, two hydrogen and one oxygen. Atoms are made of subatomic particles. The further we zoom in, the more pieces we find. There is no center to the onion.

When we drop our preconceptions, and look into anything with openness and attention, we eventually behold the place where Form is becoming Emptiness, and Emptiness is becoming Form. This is the heart of relatedness. That place is right Here. There is no adequate name for it. Attempts to name it are awkward at best—like feet on a snake. The compulsive need to understand and name things causes much confusion. Maybe it's best that we let the Unnameable remain as such.

Direct Experience

We can't find anything solid or enduring in the entire universe. We can't pin down a separate existence for ourselves. And yet we cannot deny the fact of direct experience. Experience happens; we're just not quite sure to whom. The experiencer, then, becomes less important than experience itself. Experience is tangible and reliable. It always follows natural law. Touch, taste, sight, smell, sound, thought—all are constantly changing.

A few examples. You get out of bed and walk to the bathroom in the dark. You stub your toe. There is intense sensation. You say a few profane words. The sensations last a while, and then they are gone.

You taste a mango. The flavor lingers on the tongue for a bit, then disappears. You feel the masticated fruit slide down your esophagus and enter your stomach.

You have to give an important speech this afternoon on a topic you are not an expert on. You're concerned the audience might judge you too harshly. Your solar plexus tightens up. Your heart pounds. Your hands sweat. Nothing has happened yet. You are only thinking. It's all in your mind, right? No, it's not. Body and mind are one continuum. It's all in your body-mind. Even thoughts are a whole-body experience. In all three situations, there is a mind-body experience. The basis of experience is felt-awareness. It is not merely a mental consciousness, but full body awareness.

Natural law is most tangible on the level of feeling. For human beings, the center of feeling is the belly. The center of experience is feeling. Belly, then, is the center of experience. Belly is the Center of Being.

In the Center of Being there is a river of direct experience free from the trappings of "good" and "bad." Never ending are the transformations of body and mind. Pleasant experience. Unpleasant experience. Calm mind. Racing mind. Experiences happen in a ceaseless flow of change. Each new Form arises from Emptiness and dissolves into Emptiness. Each manifestation has its own timing, and all manifestations are self-resolving.

As we begin to see clearly how nature operates, a great disillusionment dawns. The whole drama of "me as a separate entity" falls apart. The notion of an individual self, that is flawed and desperately seeking happiness, seems like a fairy tale. Like a gentle fire, this disillusionment consumes the frail need to believe in anything beyond what is immediately present in your direct experience. Hope and faith are no longer relevant. The whole of divinity is right here, originally whole, in the way things naturally unfold.

The Unburdened Heart

The root of suffering is ignorance of natural law. Thinking, speaking, or acting in disharmony with continuity, change, and interdependence produces the feeling of isolation. When we go against the natural order of things, we become refugees in our own skin. This is the abode of the *ahamkara*, the I-maker. The knot of ego-grasping is woven here. It tightens when we chase "me" and "mine." We can choose to stop chasing. It's only a habit.

When we honestly apply the art of contemplation, when we examine the nature of self with great interest, we find that nothing solid or singular exists whatsoever. We are composite, like everything else. When you see a mirage in the desert, you don't hope to be quenched by water that does not exist. Likewise, once we realize the emptiness of a solid and abiding self, we can relax the effort we've been making to fill the void. There is more space inside. The heart softens.

The "I" was never a thing. It was a thought. Between each thought, a gap. In the gaps, nobody is home. Life leaks in. The joy. The pain. All of it, felt in the raw. Awakening is a beautiful catastrophe; the whole basis of our egoistic personal agenda falls apart.

The bad news: falling can be disorienting, even downright scary. When it becomes evident that our so-called self is empty of abiding qualities, there may be a storm of anxiety. This is like the gasp reflex when one slips on an icy staircase and begins to fall.

The good news: there is nothing whatsoever to fall *into*. There is no solid ground to hit in the end. No bottom. We are openness falling into openness. As we realize there is actually no ground to land on, anxiety turns to humor. Falling becomes floating. Floating becomes walking, standing, sitting, and lying down.

These are four things we can't stop doing. Since we can't stop doing them, we make them our practice.

Anguish might be defined as making solid what is inherently open and fluid. We could describe awakening as a return from solidity to spontaneous openness—a block of ice melting into a river. If we can muster the courage to surrender into this newfound openness, we discover a warmth and luminosity that dissolves all woes. It is stated quite succinctly in the *Yoga Sutras of Patanjali* (2.16): *Heyam duhkham anagatam.* The Sanskrit phrase translates as "Future suffering is avoidable."

Future suffering *is* avoidable. The clincher is, we have to face ourselves. Many seekers hope to go beyond themselves, to sidestep the salt of their human predicament and enter a transcendent state of bliss. This is an immature fantasy. It doesn't work. Spiritual practice can easily become somewhat of an escape. There are so many gimmicks and gadgets to sidetrack us. However alluring, these serve to distract from the immediate circumstances of our life. Eventually, we have to deal with our situation.

The basis of genuine spiritual practice is self-honesty. There is no way around this. No one else can do this for you. No guru. No savior. No secret technique. No affirmation. No mantra will transport you out of your predicament. Only you can free yourself. First you must know yourself fully. Only then can you can forget yourself.

Contemplation and meditation are time-tested methods for doing this. We have to approach the whole thing with maturity and sobriety. When we honestly take up the discipline of spiritual practice, we might see how inauthentically we have been acting, how selfishly and childishly. It is easy to feel worthless. Yet we have to go deeper. We have to open the heart wider. We have to go beyond the dichotomy of self-hatred and self-aggrandizement.

"I'm awesome" and "I'm a total loser" are two sides of the same coin; both result from the habit of ego-grasping. The opinions of this so-called "inner critic" are mostly self-indulgent gossip. Seeing the absurdity of it, we smile and carry on.

When we turn within, we discover there is inherent goodness in us. It is not acquired by our effort. It is just there. Through self-reflection we learn to soften the calculated response, the clever aspect of our humanness. And, at the same time, we have a newfound confidence in basic goodness. We start to see it everywhere. Despite the morbid tone of the daily news, we start to see brightness in our life. We start to fully trust life. It is something quite different from acting optimistically. This new trust is not like hope or faith. It is based only in what we know from our direct experience. It is grounded in an intimate and ongoing relationship with reality itself.

There are endless techniques for coming to this realization. The bottom line is that we have to spend sober time with ourselves—lots of it. There is no way to bypass this. All the empowerments and *shaktipat*[12] in the world will not lessen the need for self-honesty. Spiritual busyness is a sign that we are avoiding the central point. The quest to open the chakras, raise the kundalini, advance our yoga practice, or cultivate more qi: all of this can easily lead to spiritual escapism if not accompanied by a clear understating of View.

When you think you have adequately faced yourself, there is a simple test. It takes 49 days. Sit for an hour each day and just be. During the allotted time, don't journal, don't analyze, don't plan, and don't try to fix your problems. Don't visualize. Don't "move energy." Don't chant. Don't fidget. Don't sleep. Don't move from your seat. Just sit and be. Do this seven days a week for seven weeks (49 days). This test is an honest assessment of whether or not you are facing yourself.

Embodied Presence

We have spent considerable time looking at the first two branches of our practice: exposure and contemplation. Although contemplation can bring clarity, it is easy to mistake lucid theoretical understanding for embodiment. Mental certainty of spiritual truth is quite different from realization. It takes courage to move from contemplation to embodiment. The risk of getting caught in contemplation is that one formulates lofty theories and then stands behind them, aloof from the living moment. This is a common mistake among so-called "advanced" spiritual seekers. Unchecked contemplation can render a person dharma-intoxicated. Blindly adopting spiritual axioms will do the same. This means we have taken on a particular view—usually one that espouses transcendence—and have placed that view between ourselves and the immediate situation of everyday life. Shrouded in spiritual ideals, and armed with objective understanding, a seeker can become distant from immediacy. Untouchable. This is a common obstacle on the path.

Studying an atlas is quite different from walking in the forest. At some point, we have to fold up our map of concepts and step onto the path-less path. Teachers and teachings can only point in a general direction. We have to step off and trust life itself. With the firm ground of self-honesty under our feet, a profound recognition dawns. We realize that, despite all of our learning, we actually know very little. A sense of wonder returns. Freshness. This is how self-honesty and contemplation work together. At the end of the day, contemplation clearly reveals that to satiate our innermost longing we must go beyond concepts and preconceptions. Contemplation must lead to embodiment.

Embodiment is warm and intimate, totally engaged with the immediate situation. To move from contemplation to embodiment, we have to drop our guard. The cloak of self-protecting concepts is disrobed. We become vulnerable. We feel. Contact with life reaches our bones. Embodiment means being fully alive and available. It requires that we remain open to whatever arises.

This might sound fantastic in theory. In real-life application, however, living like this can be quite confronting. It dismantles our built-up mechanisms of protection. It breaks our cover, messes with our cool. It exposes ego's hiding scheme. Nevertheless, if we are to become real human beings (Chinese *zhen ren*), we have to take the leap from contemplation to embodiment. Perhaps Dogen Zenji says it best: "Enlightenment is intimacy with all things."

The practice of the Four Dignities is precisely this: No matter what arises, let it rest in its uncontrived bare essence. Do not tamper with the natural perfection of things. Relinquish the habit of trying to improve everything, especially yourself. Let go of secret desires for exalted experience. Thoughts, emotions, sensations, memories, dreams—each arise from the matrix of inexplicable openness, last for a short duration, then dissolve into their own ground. See clearly how the multifarious appearances are self-resolving, how pristine awareness embraces all things with unwavering acceptance. Free of hopes, intentions, and lofty goals, relax into aimless Being. Walking, standing, sitting, and lying down, remain simply as you are. This is the central point.

ᛉ Chapter 2 ᚱ

ORIGINAL POSTURE

"The postures of meditation should embody steadiness and ease. This occurs as all effort relaxes and coalescence arises, revealing that the body and the infinite universe are indivisible."

Patanjali Sutras (2.46–48)

Form determines function. Original Posture is the natural form your body organizes itself in to most effectively relate with gravity. It is based on the set of dynamics that result from your unique anatomical specifications. Since no two bodies are identical, no two people have exactly the same form or function. Although there are a handful of important postural rules that support proper biomechanics, it is important to note here that Original Posture has nothing to do with conceptualized ideas of "perfect posture" or the dogmatic application of idealized rules of alignment. Such externally imposed ideas of alignment, such as those often taught in ballet, Pilates, and modern Hatha Yoga, result in a type of postural mimicking. The student visually and mentally understands the requested body position, and then employs their will to contort the body into the conceived shape. In this case, thinking instead of feeling drives the student toward a conceived goal. In the process, such a student habitually departs from naturalness and flirts with injury.

This type of postural training is useful for the attainment of a specific aesthetic or performance of a classical form. Postural mimicking reduces the differences and exaggerates the similarities among a group of people trained to move and hold their bodies in a specific way, dictated by a desired result. For a dance troop or a gymnastic class, this makes sense. However, we must be quite clear that yogic and meditative practices are developed for internal cultivation, not performance or competition. In the fostering of authentic movement and embodied Presence, postural mimicking is usually counter-productive.

Original Posture is not something we *attain* through practice. It is something we rediscover in the process of shedding layers of conditioning. Original Posture is the naked flesh beneath learned ways of holding the body.

Since form and function are intrinsically related, cultivating Original Posture is one of the foundations of our practice. A wheel with flat spots does not roll smoothly and can be dangerous at high velocity. Likewise, an improperly aligned body cannot breathe or move naturally, and, when put under the challenges of daily life, is much more likely to develop problems and unnecessary wear. While walking, standing, sitting, and lying down, we have an opportunity to cultivate our natural alignment, and to roll perhaps a bit more gracefully along life's path.

There is a dynamic way in which your bones, joints, muscles, tendons, and organs express their optimal alignment and function. There are innumerable subtle factors. For example, the length of your torso in relation to the length of your legs will influence the location of your center of gravity. The precise size and shape of your feet and femur bones affect the way you walk and sit. The width of your shoulders relative to the circumference of your ribcage affects the way your arms hang during standing and swing while walking.

Your Original Posture is closely related to how you held your body as a baby. In a sense, this postural blueprint is still in you. It can be insightful to look at photographs or video footage of yourself as an infant and toddler. See if you can find pictures or video of yourself sitting, squatting, standing, and walking. Look closely at the alignment of your head, ribcage, shoulders, spine, pelvis, and feet. This will give you an idea of the essence of your Original Posture. It is also helpful to observe babies and toddlers anytime you are around them. Notice the way they move, how their joints align, how they instinctively flow through efficient ranges of motion. Closely observing their suppleness and ease can trigger a somatic memory of your own Original Posture.

The postures of meditation are living, breathing, and constantly changing expressions. They are not fixed forms we can attain or hold on to. Embodied Presence is more like a river than a lake. There are no hard borders. Body, breath, and mind are pieces of the indivisible life matrix. Through attentiveness to the dynamic feeling of posture, we facilitate a state of relaxed alertness. This fluid moment-to-moment cultivation of Original Posture is at the root of the Four Dignities practice.

Tension and Relaxation

The body is one unit. Physically, every part of the body is encased in a unified web of connective tissue: muscles, bones, organs, nerves, and blood vessels. Information, in the form of our response to experience, is transferred across the inner webbing of connective tissue. What affects one part affects the whole. Excessive tension anywhere creates rigidity everywhere. We know that mental and emotional tension create physical tension. If we worry about something, we feel the effect in the tensing of muscles and constriction of breathing. We must also understand that physical tension generates mental and emotional tension as well.

Energetically, the body is one open space with many currents, like an ocean. In the view of Eastern self-cultivation practices, the human body is not conceived of as a thing, but as a field of experience. Mental body, emotional body, physical body, energetic body, spiritual body: these are merely linguistic differences. In reality, there is only one body, the body of direct experience. This body is not fixed or solid; it is fluid and constantly changing. Our practice is to remove tension from this body and let nature function. As always, awareness is key.

During practice of the Four Dignities, and as often as you can in everyday life, soften and relax muscular tension every time you notice it. Sometimes chronically held tension will not dissolve just because you have become aware of it. This can be frustrating for beginners. Here is where we practice a balance of relaxing and accepting. We make an invitation for relaxation, and then we fully accept and embrace whatever the immediate experience brings. Sometimes tension becomes more pronounced before it releases. Do not fight tension with disapproval or judgment. This only makes more tension. Sometimes the mental body needs to learn to relax before the physical body lets go. Acceptance. Other times the physical body has to soften before mental tension will dissolve. Suppleness.

Alignment without relaxation is rigid. Relaxation without alignment is limp. Both must be present in our practice.

Key Points of Natural Alignment

The points of alignment listed below are an invitation to listen, observe, and understand *somatically* how the body best aligns itself. It is best to esteem feeling over thinking to discover your optimal alignment and Original Posture. Pain in any joint is a sign to back off and pay closer attention. As your body sheds old patterns of tension, there may be emotional release or physical discomfort. This is a sign of physical-emotional detoxification. It is important to differentiate between the type of discomfort resulting from transformation and that which comes from an over-zealous postural correction. The former is a sign of deep healing. The latter is an indication of aggressiveness.

These points are general guidelines that apply to all Four Dignities where appropriate. For example, it is necessary to activate the arches of the feet while walking, standing, and sitting in a chair, but not while sitting cross-legged or lying down. Within the individual sections of each Dignity, additional and more specific points of alignment are also noted. Some of the points of alignment are similar or identical between Dignities. In these cases, I have noted important subtleties or attempted to reiterate essential points with fresh language.

The Feet

ACTIVATE THE ARCHES. FEEL THE EARTH.

Embodied Presence starts with consciously standing on your own two feet. The feet are your connection to the Earth. They are the essential foundation of the human body. The feet contain about one-quarter of the total number of bones in the body. One foot has 26 bones, 33 joints, and more than 100 ligaments, muscles, and tendons. The foot is a complex structure that affords a highly nuanced range of biomechanics. The feet, along with the hands and mouth, are some of the most sensitive areas of the body. With more than 7000 nerve endings, each foot gathers information about terrain, temperature, balance, and coordination. The feet work in harmony with the central nervous system to optimize systemic function. Natural alignment and stimulation of the feet benefits the whole body, including the function of all the internal organs.

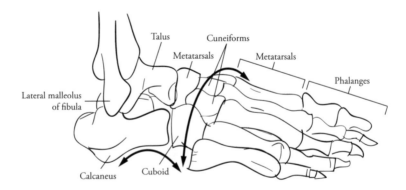

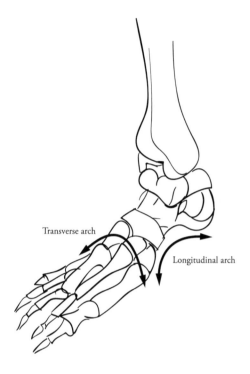

Transverse arch

Longitudinal arch

The most effective way to encourage proper alignment and healthy function of the feet is to go barefoot. An entire volume could be dedicated to the importance of restoring your feet back to their native function. This would entail a more comprehensive understanding of the anatomy and physiology of the feet, shoe choices, foot exercises, barefoot walking, and so on. Since this is not the specific focus here, we will simple say that, for the practice of the Four Dignities, it is imperative that the feet be liberated from their shoes whenever possible.

Practicing barefoot will stimulate the natural intelligence of the feet. What might take many hours to learn from a teacher will start to occur naturally. Namely, the bones of the feet will begin to spread and the natural arches of the foot—transverse and longitudinal—will wake up. Furthermore, the strength and sensitivity of the feet will come alive. And the life-supporting current of Vital Force will flow more smoothly from the Earth into the body. Awakening the feet enlivens Presence through the whole body.

The saying "to have both feet on the ground" is both literal and metaphoric. Literally, it means actually feeling the ground beneath one's feet. We might say such a person is *actively* standing. Metaphorically, the saying implies that such a person is in touch with reality, engaged with the circumstances at hand. Conversely, one who has "their head in the clouds" clearly does not have "both feet on the ground." To foster physical and emotional balance, as well as spiritual development, it is paramount to become more aware of your feet and their relationship with the Earth.

The Knees
MAINTAIN COORDINATION OF THE FEET, KNEES, AND HIPS.

The knees are perhaps the most basic and hard-working of all the joints. The knee is a simple hinge joint. It does not respond well to torsion or lateral pressure. Proper functioning of the knees is largely affected by the position of the feet and hips. If the arches of the feet collapse, the knee falls out of alignment. If the connective tissue around the hips becomes too tight or loose, the knees wander from their ideal position.

The key to maintaining natural alignment of the knees is to feel the coordination that happens between the hips, knees, and feet. It is helpful to imagine a line running vertically through the front-center of the thigh, the middle of the kneecap, and the center of the foot. In walking, standing, sitting, and lying down, it is important to maintain alignment of these three along the same line.

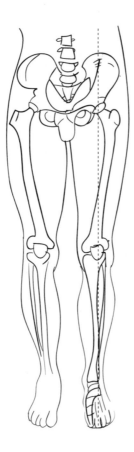

In the beginning, you may need to check this line repeatedly by looking down and visually tracing from the center of the thigh to the foot. With time, you will be able to feel this relationship without needing to look. As with many aspects of our practice, the ability to feel is what matters most. If we learn to "listen" to our knees, they will dictate the more subtle postural adjustments necessary for optimal alignment. When the hips, knees, and feet operate in unison, there is a sense of natural comfort.

The Pelvis

MAINTAIN A NEUTRAL PELVIS.

There is no need to strongly tuck or tip the pelvis. Doing so creates unnecessary tension and inhibits Original Posture. The safest and most natural position of the pelvis is neutral. Ironically, the neutral position can be the most challenging position to feel. When the pelvis is in the neutral position, there is relatively little gross muscular sensation. To begin exploring where neutral actually is, tuck and tip the pelvis through the full range of motion. During tucking, the tailbone moves down and forward, and the small of the back becomes flat. During tipping, the tailbone lifts up and back, the pubic bone drops down, and the curve of the lower back exaggerates. Continue tucking and tipping, making each movement smaller and smaller until you reach the position that feels most neutral. In the neutral pelvic position, the lumbar curve is noticeable, but not exaggerated.

Maintenance of neutral pelvic alignment is the foundation of a strong, supple, resilient body. Learning to feel the natural alignment of the pelvis can take time. Some people may take years to unwind layers of subtle tension from the pelvis and finally discover their Original Posture. For many, it can be an emotional journey. However, with careful attention and patience, you may find a sense of ease in the pelvis after a brief time. Each of us must walk our own path. There is no rush. There are no short cuts. To fully embody our Original Posture, awareness must permeate the pelvis. This step cannot be skipped.

The Belly

REST IN THE CENTER OF BEING.

The feelings of alienation, separateness, anxiety, and loneliness that are so common in our society arise from a departure from the Center of Being. Lost in constant self-critique, and addicted to passive entertainment, our culture treads on the brink of spiritual oblivion. The solution is simple: move the feeling of identity, the sense of "I," from the head to the lower belly. While centered in the belly, one feels intimately connected to everything that is happening. There is an innate sense of Presence and basic joy. One's value is no longer in question. No amount of mental posturing can produce this feeling. No amount of analyzing can lead one to this realization. It is a matter of relaxing effort, feeling, and allowing awareness to sink down into the lower belly.

The Center of Being is not something that can be observed objectively. Just as the eye cannot see itself, the subject cannot be made into an object. To activate belly-centered Presence, one needs only to release the strength from every other part of the body and let it return to the Center. This is done by very subtly activating the musculature of the pelvic floor and lower abdomen, while simultaneously softening every other part of the body, especially the shoulders.

The Spine

MAINTAIN LENGTH. PRESERVE THE
THREE SPINAL CURVES.

The spine is the central column upholding the beautiful architecture of the human form. From the tip of the tailbone to the crown of the head, always maintain a sense of length and spaciousness. This harvests the force of gravity, reduces compression, and allows each of the 24 vertebrae to find their natural position. Length and space allow the spinal column to function as a dynamic whole. There is no need to exaggerate the "straightness" of the spine. Images of the Buddha sitting ramrod straight are exaggerated for aesthetic purposes. Real spines have curves. By simply maintaining a sense of length, the three spinal curves—lumbar, thoracic, and cervical—will find their optimal shape and function.

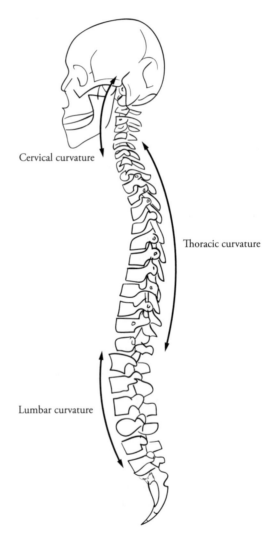

Cervical curvature

Thoracic curvature

Lumbar curvature

The Shoulders

LET THEM FALL AWAY FROM THE EARS.

Chronic tension in the shoulders is a product of the age of anxiety. It is a sign that we are overusing our personal will and overemphasizing the value of ambition. When we get caught up in the "I must conquer the world" way of thinking, our shoulders ride up and our breathing becomes shallow. This incites the fight-or-flight response and produces feelings of inner conflict and claustrophobia. The solution is twofold: mental and physical. First, it is necessary to contemplate View teachings and practice self-reflection. Anxious effort always hinges on a set of unchecked assumptions. Remember, the way you do things is dependent on the way you see the world. When you remember the principle of intrinsic wholeness, you can relax and act in harmony with nature. Second, you must learn to consciously relax the musculature around the jaw, neck, and shoulders. Simply soften from within and let the shoulders fall. It may be helpful to imagine the feeling of a silk cape sliding down your shoulders and back.

Finding the Original Posture of the shoulders is a matter of relaxing and getting out of the way. You might notice the shoulders riding up a hundred times during one session of practice. Don't get frustrated. Actively pressing the shoulders down is much too aggressive, and usually results in further tension. Whenever you notice a tensing of the shoulders, or any part of the body, employ patience and gentleness. With time, awareness, and diligent practice, the habit of tensing will dissolve.

The Arms

LET THEM HANG.

The upright spine of the human body dictates that the arms are meant to hang at the sides. Habitually holding the arms and shoulders up taxes the muscles of the neck and upper back. This spreads tension through the body, creating fixation in the tissues. Fixation, or constant contraction, deters the flow of blood and vital energy. Tension in the arms and shoulders changes the movement of the ribcage and distorts the natural breath cycle. The antidote is to simply allow the arms to hang free and easy at all times. Gravity is a wonderful assistant. Feel as though the arms are sliding off the body, falling toward the floor.

The Head

RELAX THE BRAIN. KEEP A COOL HEAD.

"Keep the head cool and the belly warm." This is a poignant saying often taught in Asian martial arts and meditative traditions. For physical health and spiritual wellbeing, it is one of the most valuable pieces of advice you can receive. "Keeping a cool head" is a matter of learning to calm the habit of excessive mental busyness. Physically, one must learn to soften the brain, eyes, and jaw, and keep the head in line with the vertical axis. Energetically, the fire of Presence has to descend from the head to its rightful home in the belly. "Keeping the belly warm" is a matter of relaxing the abdomen and feeling the center of gravity shift to a lower point. When the head is cool and aligned, and the belly is warm, a natural sense of comfort and vitality permeates body and mind.

The Teeth

LIGHTLY TOUCHING.

During practice of the Four Dignities, the mouth remains closed with the teeth lightly touching. The muscles of the jaw and mouth stay relaxed and soft. This allows the breathing to happen through the nose, and maintains the natural structure of the skull and neck.

The Tongue

FILLS THE MOUTH.

Keep the tongue gently lifted, lightly touching the upper palate. The tongue then relaxes and fills the space inside the mouth. Swallow and feel what the tongue does. Maintain this relaxed position of the tongue. This will keep the mouth free of tension and reduce the need to frequently swallow saliva during meditation.

The Eyes

SOFTEN THE GAZE. REST IN LUMINOUS SPACE.

During practice of the Four Dignities, keep the eyes soft and receptive. They do not need to be fully open or completely closed. You can relax the need for intense focused concentration with the mind and eyes (*yang*). Allow the eyes to simply rest in space. In this way, you receive the world passively (*yin*). Learning to make this shift from *yang* to *yin* is deeply nourishing for body and mind. When the eyes become passive, a harmony occurs between "inside" and "outside." This allows the Vital Force to flow more freely through the body.

Opening the Spiritual Gates

There are more than 230 movable and semi-movable joints in the human body. Joints are created by the convergence of bones where cartilage, ligaments, tendons, nerves, and blood vessels work in cooperation. Each joint serves as a bridge, linking the nerves and vessels that make up the body's vast communication network. The space between bones is quite similar to the space between the individual neurons, called the synaptic cleft, that make up the vast network of our nervous system.

The joints of the body are like precious pearls. All of our body's movements depend on healthy function of the joints. Ancient Daoists used the term "spiritual gates" to describe the body's joints. Through conscious movement and deep meditation, they discovered that the flow of Vital Force through the body is largely dependent on the "openness" of the joints. Openness means that there is ample space between bones, and the natural movement of breath is free to ripple through these spaces. If there is excess tension in the muscles or abdominal organs, our breathing becomes restricted, the spaces between the bones gets smaller, and the joints lock up.

Opening the spiritual gates is not a matter of becoming overly flexible. In fact, excessive stretching can expand the range of motion of the joints too much. The joints and surrounding tissues then tense up as a mechanism of protection. I have seen this happen many times with over-zealous practitioners of Hatha Yoga. Gentle stretching is beneficial for the muscles, fascia, and nervous system, yet the key to opening the spiritual gates is somatic awareness and natural breathing. When relaxed attention permeates all the joints, we experience a sense of inner luminosity.

Being in proper alignment with open joints means that the bones, muscles, tendons, and ligaments can do their job in supporting the body in relationship to gravity. In natural posture, the internal organs rest in their proper place and all is in good order. We are going for normal function of the human system, nothing extraordinary. In all Four Dignities, we want to keep the joints "open" and all the muscles soft and supple. Opening the joints means growing the space between the bones. We want to do this in every joint of the body. Natural alignment is the essential foundation by which we cultivate good health, flexibility, suppleness, lightness, and vigor. A naturally aligned body is a suitable abode for a calm and alert spirit.

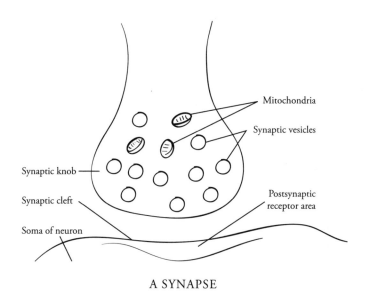

Mitochondria

Synaptic vesicles

Synaptic knob

Synaptic cleft

Postsynaptic
receptor area

Soma of neuron

A SYNAPSE

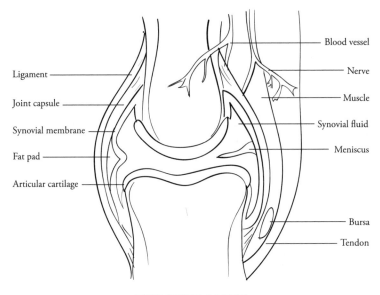

Ligament

Joint capsule

Synovial membrane

Fat pad

Articular cartilage

Blood vessel

Nerve

Muscle

Synovial fluid

Meniscus

Bursa

Tendon

THE KNEE JOINT

Heaven, Earth, and Human Being

We have indicated key points of alignment to consider within the body. Now let us move beyond the borders of our skin to gain a wider view. The expanded picture of Original Posture includes our relationship with what is above, below, and all around us. Under our feet, Earth is solid and reliable. Above our head, the sky is constantly changing. In a broader sense, alignment also means maintaining an intimate relationship with the natural world. There is no special knowledge needed to do this. It happens automatically when we relax our fixed ideas of what "I" am. An intuitive sense looms into view: that Heaven, Earth and Human Being are one continuum.

The seasons change as Earth journeys around the Sun. The Moon traces an ever-changing arc across the sky. Constellations appear to revolve around the North Star. On the macrocosmic level, celestial bodies move around magnetic centers. When we practice the Four Dignities, our magnetic center is felt as the central axis of our body. This is the imaginary line running from the crown of the head through the core of the body to the pelvic floor, then down into the feet. Asian traditions often refer to this as the central channel.[13] When we remain open and relaxed along the central axis, we discover that our experience of body does not end at the edge of our skin. As a field of energy-experience, pure being has no clear borders. Heaven, Earth, and Human are terms of convention, not true distinctions. In the microcosm of our direct experience, we discover body and mind express the continuity of all things.

The notion that "all things are my body" is quite abstract for the rational mind to grasp. There is not much else we can say to clarify. Actually, it is not important that we understand this intellectually. Nor is it a matter of needing to believe, or trying to expand our circle of identification. The point of mentioning this at all is so we know this experience is something practitioners pass through along the Way.

At some point in your practice, if it has not happened already, you will feel the continuity of Heaven, Earth, and Human. It's as if you can't quite tell where "you" end and "everything else" begins. It is important not to get too excited when this happens. The temptation to talk with others about your revelation can be quite strong. It is best to keep the experience to yourself. And if you must, speak only with your teacher or mentor to clarify any confusion. Also, don't let your mind make it a goal to achieve or repeat this experience. It is not an objective or a sign of "progress." Ego-grasping loves to take on expanded identifications. Thinking "I am everything" is a mistake. Thinking "I am nothing" is also a mistake. We just keep practicing.

As conceptual identifications fall away, the nature of things becomes evident in our experience. We then know clearly that we are not what we think; we are not anything that can be conceived. Experiencing the unity of Heaven, Earth, and Human is another opportunity to honestly admit, "I don't know." This sincere feeling of "I don't know" is the only foolproof way to open the central channel and reside in the dimension of primordial Being.

Harvesting Gravity

In all of the Four Dignities, we experience a palpable downward force pulling toward Earth. Gravity. We know it exists, and we know its constant influence is relentless: slipping on a wet tile floor, dropping a cell phone, knocking over a cup of hot tea. Gravity is so much a part of our daily life that it is easy to overlook its importance.

Newton explained gravity in a clean and tidy way: a force pulling toward the center of the Earth. Then Einstein came along and turned the Newtonian idea of gravity on its head. He explained that gravity is a product of the curvature of space. Bodies are not acted upon directly by a force exerted on them, but they are compelled to bend along with the curvature of space. Gravity is a phenomenon that continues to cause even the most cutting-edge scientists to scratch their heads. A theory of quantum gravity is in the works, yet much remains unclear. Science is certain gravity exists, but we still know very little about exactly how it functions in the larger view of things.

Let us turn for a moment to a simple observation about gravity made by ancient yogis. For a person interested in discovering greater vitality and fulfillment, gravity is studied not by means of instruments or mathematical equations, but within the domain of direct experience. Using body and mind as the laboratory, yogis understood that gravity was a constant force. As such, they sought to cultivate an active relationship with gravity that assisted their practice. They treated gravity as one of the many observable expressions of cosmic energy (*prana*, *qi*, *ki*). They found that gravity could be "harvested" to support the health of body and mind. They explained that gravity's obvious effect was experienced as the downward pull toward the Earth. They described this as descending energy. They also noticed another, perhaps more subtle, responsive force going the opposite direction. They called this rising energy.

Conventionally, we know that there is a reactive force corresponding to gravity. Visualize a falling object, say a ball. Once it hits the floor, it will bounce back up a certain distance, depending on its weight, speed, density, and so on. What yogis discovered is that this reactive force is also operative in objects as they remain in contact with Earth—namely the human body. Because there is a constant "falling" of the body, there is also a corresponding "bouncing up." This is going on even when our feet don't leave the ground.

This is not observed visually as an up-and-down movement, but felt inwardly more like the movement of gentle winds. Yogis found that rising and descending energies are in perfect balance in the natural world. Rain falls down to Earth. Water in a pond evaporates up to Heaven. These corresponding movements are the basis of circulation. The same rising and falling energies are moving in and through our bodies. This creates a constantly self-renewing flow of Vital Force. Through awareness, proper alignment, and natural breathing, we harmonize with this circulatory flow of energy.

Gravity's constant downward pull is a big help for the meditation practitioner. By its nature, gravity can pull even the subtlest of things downward. With Original Posture, even thoughts will "descend" to a lower center. The head becomes lighter and the belly more stable. In the practice of all Four Dignities, we allow gravity to guide the feeling of Being to a lower point. Gravity assists our journey from identification with thinking (head) to Presence (belly). As we relax and notice this descending quality, the corresponding ascending property has a spontaneously uplifting effect. If we try to lift ourselves up artificially, we disconnect from gravity. This produces, at best, a faint imitation of lightness. Genuine lightness comes from being grounded. This rule applies physically, mentally, emotionally, and so on.

Chapter 3

ORIGINAL BREATH

"Awareness of the life manifest in breathing is present in reality only when one senses the Great Respiration and finally he keeps in rhythm with it. This means yielding oneself without reservation to the cosmic movement of ebb and flow."

Karlfried Graf Dürckheim

Proper breathing is an act of permitting the exhale to depart unaltered, and allowing the inhale to arrive of itself. All other yogic breathing practices eventually lead us to this. As our practice matures, the process of breathing teaches us how we might give up the habit of micromanaging our natural response—the result of clutching to notions of a separate and fixed self. Life has breathing handled! When we trust this and truly surrender, we discover a more free and open way of breathing and being.

There is a Chinese saying, "A baby breathes from the belly, an adult from the chest, an elderly person from the throat, and a dying person from the mouth." This poignant aphorism directs our attention to some essential connections between breathing, psychology, aging, and vitality. For anyone sincerely interested in self-healing and spiritual cultivation, a thorough investigation into the nuances of proper breathing is indispensable.

Babies are not conscious of their own breathing. When the life-breath moves through a baby's body, it meets no resistance. Babies bubble over with vitality. They do not try to breathe deeply, yet their breath is full and powerful. However, as babies grow and become more aware, they begin to mimic the older kids and adults around them. Unconsciously, they contort their posture and breathing little by little, year by year, to mirror the social norm. Tragically, what has become "normal" posture and breathing in industrialized cultures is far from what is natural. Nevertheless, our young people mimic what is all around them.

By the time most modern children reach 11 or 12 years old, they have become habituated to tensing their abdomen and breathing shallowly, primarily from the upper chest. Girls learn to "suck it in," and boys are taught to "suck it up." These notions are affirmed time and time again through advertising and popular imagery. Tension in the solar plexus accompanies chest breathing and contributes to anxiety, difficulty concentrating, and digestive complications. This type of breathing overstimulates the sympathetic nervous system, clicking on the fight-or-flight response.

Once kids hit puberty, the conditioned patterns of posture and breathing become even more pronounced. Like the adults all around them, they have learned to be uncomfortable in their own skin. Modern medicine diagnoses the more prominent cases with newly fashioned syndromes treated with customized pharmaceutical drugs. Yet the root of the problem remains unresolved.

Patterns of tension and inner conflict can be seen in one's posture and heard in the rhythm of respiration. The body does not lie. Teens are not yet sophisticated enough to cover up their uneasiness and conceal their turmoil. Their feelings come out charged and raw. The adults around them usually meet this uncensored display of emotion with disapproval. Judgment further evokes conflict; thus the need to rebel. Teens desperately want to avoid becoming like the adults they see. Still pure of heart, they despise hypocrisy and loathe the way adults mask their true face and misuse their authority.

Sadly, teens are not yet wise enough to avoid following in society's footsteps. As they mature into adults, they develop a sophisticated personal façade used to conceal their feelings and present the "proper face." It is terribly common that by adulthood most modern people have begrudgingly accepted shallow breathing, inauthenticity, and the incessant pursuit of sensory gratification in an attempt to soothe the inner discontentment with it all. This private discomfort is a driving force behind our culture's desperate need for distraction. Yet, alas, nothing acquired from the outside removes our uneasiness. Nobody forgets the truth; we just get better at lying to ourselves.

The inner yearning to breathe easy and be at home in your own skin can be hushed, but never silenced. It is always there in the background: that quiet whisper behind everything you do, the odd sense that perhaps some part of yourself has been misplaced. Yet not one single thing is lacking. Here-and-now you are whole and complete, as always. It is just that you have been taught to move, breathe, and be like someone you are not. The angry teenager might still be there, hidden behind an adult's refined face.

For most of us, estrangement from Being probably started in early childhood. They told you how to be. They told you how to think, how to eat, how to sit. Unaware that no model from the outside could teach you how to be what you naturally are, parents, coaches, teachers, and religious leaders likely misled you. You temporarily lost track of your Original Breath. But it did not lose track of you. Like Original Posture, your Original Breath is in your bones, in your DNA. You couldn't get away from it if you tried. The breath you breathed as a baby is right here, concealed in your very flesh. As the old Daoists would say, "the secret is behind the paper door." Which is to say, the secret of Original Breath is scarcely hidden at all. Poke your finger thought the paper and look right at it.

Those who would attend to the inner calling, and walk the path of self-cultivation, must remember the baby's easy inhales and exhales. Such a person must reclaim their indigenous way of breathing. Original Breath is about breath freedom. It is about liberating conditioned patterns of body and mind and allowing the Vital Force to operate unchecked. No special training in breathing is necessary. In fact, dropping the willful need to assist or control the breath through learned techniques (pranayama, etc.) is a prerequisite for rediscovering your Original Breath. Specific ways of breathing learned from outside and understood by the intellect are always limited. The mind will never fully understand the mystery of Great Respiration: how the universe breathes, how the life force animates all things. In fact, willfully manipulating our breathing causes subtle tension and feeds the ego-driven need for control. As it turns out, surrender is the final frontier for the spiritual seeker interested in the power of breath.

Original Breath happens by itself, like the beating of your heart. It is essential to allow your breathing to respond to the demands of each situation and the changing metabolic needs of the body. This is what we call trusting in Original Breath. Natural breathing happens through the nose. During the practice of the Four Dignities, we keep the mouth closed. The inhale then arrives of itself. The exhale departs unaltered. As the inhale arrives, we don't count it as a gain. When the exhale departs, we don't count it as a loss.

This might seem obvious, yet there is an underlying subtlety that warrants further inspection. If you are reluctant to let the "outside world" in, you might notice a kind of physical and mental tension limiting your inhalation. If you harbor any fear of letting go, you will likely notice the exhalation is incomplete. This reluctance to allow for a complete exhale usually coincides with constipation and tight muscles. There is a psycho-spiritual component to holding on. These are a few of the important indicators that tell the story of how breathing interconnects the physical, mental, emotional, and spiritual dimensions of our experience.

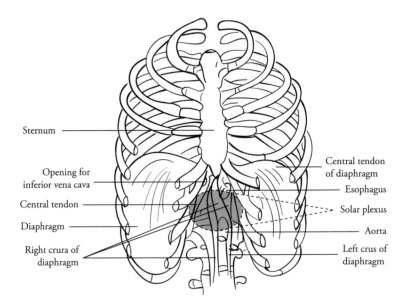

Sternum

Opening for
inferior vena cava

Central tendon

Diaphragm

Right crura of
diaphragm

Central tendon
of diaphragm

Esophagus

Solar plexus

Aorta

Left crus of
diaphragm

There is a secret cavern between the sternum and the navel. It is sometimes called the solar plexus. When we soften and breathe more fully here, we discover greater calm and newfound vitality. Perhaps more important than any chakra or energy center, this area holds the key to re-establishing Original Breath. If you can maintain softness and openness here while walking, standing, sitting, and lying down, you will have thoroughly reawakened Original Breath. This limitless breathing is the unwavering support behind all that you do. It is your direct connection to the Vital Force. By cultivating Original Breath and Original Posture, you will find yourself in the Center of Being and discover a greater sense of ease and joy in all that you do.

※ Chapter 4 ※

ORIGINAL NATURE

"Tension is who you think you should be. Relaxation
is who you are."

Chinese Proverb

Initially, we come to spiritual practice seeking personal benefit.
Not fully satisfied with our experience, we want an upgrade.
Like so many before us, we came to the Path seeking truth and
transcendence. We wanted to go beyond a limited capacity for
procuring happiness. We wanted a greater power to see our
desires met. We wanted to erase unfavorable circumstances and
secure unwavering satisfaction. And, perhaps without knowing
it, we were looking for a way out of the oppressive tyranny of
self-critique. For these reasons and many more, we start seeking.

The basic energy behind seeking is the essence of authentic
spiritual practice. It comes from a spark of non-knowing. It is

a grope in the dark, full of promise. Seeking, in its inception, is purely open and unguarded. Yet, as soon as a little knowledge is acquired, "I" uses it to strengthen self-identity. The so-called "spiritual ego" is born. Ego is really an inadequate term for describing the multifaceted habit of identification. Ego is not a noun, but a verb. It is the action of grasping. It is the dire need to be something certain and concrete, to be self-assured. Yet the basic ground of our experience, if we are completely honest with ourselves, is an overwhelming sense of "I don't know." We don't know what we are. We don't know what's going on here. We don't know the future, or fully understand the past. Like a huge black hole smack in the center of our experience, "I don't know" is always looming. It scares the shit out of us.

Ego-grasping is a knee-jerk attempt to make "I don't know" go away. The main tactic is to latch on to identities, to try to become something specific, something tangible. It's easy to turn to religion, science, mythology, or spirituality for a story to soothe the ache of non-knowing. These can be beautiful and artistic ways of expressing the great unknowable if we avoid the trap of identification. Yet strong identification with characteristic ways of acting and thinking can easily distract us from the nagging fact that we don't know what we are. To block the sting of it, we construct something out of nothing. The "I" is born. Then we desperately try to make that "I" happy by strengthening the sense of "me," and growing the wealth of "mine." Nevertheless, our attempts to hide behind a robust sense of "I" are in vain.

"Me" is a bundle of composite identifications. "Mine" are the beliefs, people, places, and things we clutch to and think we own. "I," "me," and "mine" are the warp, weft, and loom from which the great illusion is woven. The root of ignorance and suffering is the unchecked notion of an abiding self in desperate need of happiness or enlightenment. We pull the wool over our own eyes by not checking to see if any such thing as an abiding self exists in the first place. There is a great deal of anxiety and aggression in the whole thing. Grasping. Hoping. Wanting. The heroic quest for enlightenment. Gurus. Initiation. The whole drama of it. The desire for spiritual attainment is an expression of ego-grasping. It can be quite tricky to see this in ourselves. It takes considerable courage to admit we're grasping. We can cloak ego-grasping in exotic names and adorn it with mala beads, yet the point still remains.

Original Nature cannot be attained. Everything that is pitched as a benefit of spiritual practice is already inherent in Original Nature. Purification, cleverness, technique, and transmission—all are superfluous in approaching the heart of basic joy. Silently, behind even our most noble spiritual pursuits, intrinsic freedom is ever-present. Enjoyment is the ground of existence. It can only be reached by relaxing and letting things take their course. Nobody can give that to you. Nobody can take it away. Original Nature is rediscovered by saying "no" to the habit of striving for improved experience. As the old saying goes, "don't kick up dust." Even the subtle notion of goal-oriented spiritual practice serves to kick up dust, which temporarily obscures Original Nature.

It is quite liberating to reflect on the fact that what we seek from spiritual practice is innate. Yet, at the same time, this is disturbing news for the habit of ego-driven aspiration. The "spiritual ego" does not like to hear that its efforts have been for naught. Each practitioner eventually comes to this crossroads. Fully realizing the error of grasping gives rise to the Great Disillusionment. The typical progress-oriented approach to spirituality falls apart. We find the treasure of self-fulfilled Being behind the doorway of "I don't know." Honestly admitting "I don't know what I am" is a prerequisite for returning to Original Nature. When we think we know what will make us happy, we chase it. Both material and spiritual attainments produce, at best, a temporary rush of satisfaction. Yet this peak always subsides, followed by an equally intense dip. It's like coming home from a meditation retreat, or completing a month-long yoga teacher training. Highs are always accompanied by lows. Both are temporary. Our practice is to discover what is constant, and to express this in everyday life.

When Desire Fulfills Itself

When we desire things, they appear desirable. When we relax desire, things appear as-they-are. The irony is that Original Nature cannot be attained by desiring it. Until one admits, "I don't know how to get happy," the habit of chasing an upgraded experience continues. Interest in lofty goals indicates discontentment with what-is. Material fantasy and spiritual fantasy are one and the same. Enlightenment will no sooner solve your problems than a facelift and a new Mercedes-Benz. Whatever can be gained will also be lost. Again, Original Nature cannot be attained.

Do you remember the three dying wishes of Alexander the Great? One, "my physicians must carry my coffin to my grave." Two, "the path to my grave is to be decorated with my riches." And three, "my hands are to be left dangling outside my coffin." Puzzled by such unorthodox requests, his generals asked for an explanation. "Staring death in the eye today, I have learned three important lessons," Alexander said. "My physicians will carry my coffin so all will understand that even the best doctors cannot keep a man alive when his time comes. Gold, silver, and jewels will adorn the path to my grave so all will know that whatever acquired in this life is merely on loan. And by leaving my hands outside my coffin, the people will know that all men come into this world empty-handed, and leave the same way."

Who knows if Alexander actually uttered such things on his dying days? History or mythology, it really doesn't matter. The story has relevance to all of us. It contains important pointers for those who would honestly take up the Path. Even if the "I" could swell its magnitude of influence and acquisition to match that of Alexander the Great, we die empty-handed.

The great secret of spiritual practice is that what we seek is indigenous to us. Even with empty hands, it is here. It is the comprehensiveness of our experience that we are interested in. Totality. Not "this" over "that." Not ups over downs. Not light versus dark. Original Nature is the resolution of opposites. It is the common ground of all experience.

The practice of the Four Dignities is to simply walk, stand, sit, and lie down while maintaining Original Posture, Original Breath, and Original Nature. Posture is cultivated by dropping learned ways of holding the body. Breath is found by stepping out of the way and allowing ourselves to be breathed by life. Nature comes forth when we return to the unavoidable suchness of what we are. There is no need for formal rules, strict moral guidelines, long-winded sermons, or stick-enforced punishments. No glory. No guilt. No heaven. No hell. We practice because there is an inclination to do so. It is the continuity of our practice that counts. Practice itself is the result we seek.

Water flows. Fire burns. The Sun shines. Spiritual practitioners practice. Original Nature is just this. While walking, just walk. While standing, just stand. While sitting, just sit. While lying down, just be where you are. Original Nature is most ordinary. Don't make a big deal of it. When we live from this Center of

Being, there are no trivial movements. Making an important career decision, making passionate love to your partner, standing in line at the grocery store, removing hair from the shower drain—all are carried out with the same sense of importance. Each moment is a type of fullness. Mind-fullness. Heart-fullness. If we live this way, each circumstance is complete unto itself. Fulfillment is found here-and-now.

This is Original Nature.

Part II

METHOD

"Walk like the wind. Stand like a pine tree. Sit like a bell. Lie down like a bow."

Daoist Proverb

Now that we have discussed the View informing the Four Dignities, it is time to put our understanding into physical practice. In this section, we dive into the practical application of walking, standing, sitting, and lying down. We look closely at these four activities and develop an appreciation for the unique posture, alignment, breathing, and awareness essential to each. We discover the secrets of how these four can be used to cultivate embodied Presence and awaken the latent self-healing powers of body and mind.

The essence of the practice is to maintain Original Posture, Original Breath, and Original Nature while walking, standing, sitting, and lying down. When we move, breathe, and act in accord with our intrinsic way of being, we discover an ever-present sense of connectedness and vitality.

In terms of self-healing, softening your belly and allowing your breathing to be full and unlabored will do more for your health than any super-food or special supplement. When the Vital Force triggers your thrive reflex,[14] spontaneous healing happens at the deepest levels of your being.

Chapter 5

WALKING

"Keep walking though there's no place to get to."

Rumi

Walking is perhaps the most quintessential of all human movements. The upright spine, with its three signature curves, lends itself to a particular type of locomotion unique to human beings. The size and shape of the human pelvis, relative to the femur bones and spinal column, allows us to move with uncanny poise and grace. Our gait is a miraculous coordination of hundreds of bones and joints working in unison with muscles, tendons, ligaments, and nerves. Walking creates a cadenced pattern that moves in waves and spirals through every tissue of the body. This, along with the rhythmic movement established by natural breathing, facilitates the smooth circulation of blood and vital energy to every part of the body.

The dynamics of walking form the blueprint of all yogic movement, dance, and martial arts. Walking offers the perfect blend of simplicity and highly nuanced biomechanics. No special equipment or athletic skills are needed. And yet the endless subtleties of walking make it the ideal form of movement for training in embodied Presence. As we learn to feel and breathe through the whole body, walking meditation also becomes a powerful method of self-healing and health maintenance.

The benefits of walking meditation are extolled in Daoist, Buddhist, and Indian Yogic traditions. The Pali Canon, one of the oldest collections of early Buddhist writings, gives a detailed description of the profound merits of walking. The *Cankama Sutta* (5.29) reads:

> These are the five rewards for one who practices walking meditation. He can endure traveling long distances by foot; he can endure exertion; he becomes free from disease; whatever he has eaten and drunk, chewed and savored, becomes well-digested; the concentration he wins while doing walking meditation lasts for a long time. These are the five rewards for one who practices walking meditation.

The benefits described above cover a wide range of influence: physical, mental, energetic, and spiritual. Walking takes on a unique importance among the Four Dignities because it entails movement. Walking meditation is a practice of stillness in motion. The other three Dignities—standing, sitting, and lying down— are practices of motion in stillness. In walking, the experience of movement is more obvious while the quality of stillness is subtler. In the other three Dignities, the quality of stillness is primary. The underlying quality of movement is subtly felt in the rhythm of breathing and circulation of blood and vital energy.

Discovering Walking Meditation

Walking is employed as a form of spiritual cultivation in many traditions. I first discovered walking meditation in college while practicing at a local Zen center. In the Japanese Zen Buddhist tradition, walking meditation is called *Kinhin* ("sutra walking"). It is usually practiced in groups and is highly formalized to keep order and continuity. It is practiced between sessions of seated meditation (*zazen*) and has a wide range of pace. *Kinhin* is practiced indoors at slower paces, sometimes so slowly that each step takes one full breath cycle. When practiced outside, *Kinhin* usually moves a bit faster, ranging from normal walking to running.

Aboriginal cultures use walking as part of the vision quest process for warriors and shaman, and as a rite of passage for boys becoming men. While in Eastern Ecuador, on the outskirts of the Amazon jungle, I had the good fortune of meeting and studying with a local shaman. On a multi-day walkabout through the jungle, he explained to me that his tribe used walking to develop spiritual connectedness. He taught me that his people believed we have to know ourselves to know the jungle. We must learn to blend with the jungle, to feel it as an extension of our body. We walk *with* the jungle, not *in* it. "In this way," he said, "we enter into harmony with ourselves and the surroundings." He told me this is how his people could navigate the thick tropical forest, find food and shelter, and avoid the many dangers of the Amazon.

He went on to explain that his own son had recently undergone a test as part of his passage into manhood. His son was blindfolded, taken into a remote part of the jungle, and left there alone with no food, water, tools, or weapons. His test was simple: make it back to the village alive. To pass the test, he had to apply his tribe's teachings on walking, feeling, blending, and trusting the inner light of awareness. The shaman smiled proudly as he recounted the conclusion of the story. His son—who was sitting by his father's side catching fireflies and putting them in my hand while his dad told the story—apparently made it home faster than anybody else the tribe could remember.

"The real miracle is not to walk on water or in thin air, but to walk upon the Earth."

Thich Nhat Hanh

On the same trip to South America in 1996, I discovered a small commune of Daoist monks and nuns living in the remote mountain region of Santander, Colombia. I had been practicing qigong and yoga in a city park. After my session, some high school kids approached me to ask what I was doing. After some time chatting, they told me about some people they called *Los Daoistas* who lived in the mountains. At first I thought they were joking. Daoists in Colombia? Nevertheless, I was intrigued.

I took a bus to the region they told me about. On the long bumpy ride, I asked passengers if they had heard of *Los Daoistas*. A few people confirmed they had heard of them and that I was on the right bus. The driver stopped on the side of the road in what seemed like the middle of nowhere. He smiled and indicated that this was my stop. I grabbed my backpack and got off the bus. It was still a couple of hours before sundown.

To my left was a long dirt road leading into the forest. To my right was a small wooden hut near a roadside creek. I walked up to the hut and was greeted by a long-haired gentleman dressed in loose black cotton ceremonial-looking clothes. He looked uncharacteristic for the region. He must have been about 50 years old. His demeanor was calm and radiant. He smiled and welcomed me inside. We talked for a while in Spanish. There were long pauses. He seemed comfortable with his aloneness, yet it was clear he was happy to have some company. I asked him about *Los Daoistas*. It turned out he was one of them. "Yes, yes, you can go there in the morning. It's a long walk," he said. "Today it is too late to go. You can stay here with me."

While he prepared dinner, we listened to a tape-recorded lecture of one of his Daoist teachers. The voice billowed out of an old scratchy handheld stereo. The speaker was discussing Daoist philosophy and self-cultivation. The simple meal consisted of fresh-baked bread and a special soup made of *borojó* fruit. The food was delicious. As we ate, he explained that the *borojó* fruit has special properties that boost a man's virility. He made a fist and held his forearm vertical, forming the universal male power gesture. "*Como así*," he said. "Like this." We both laughed. He went on to explain that Daoists eat certain foods and do specific practices to strengthen their life energy and promote spiritual growth. While cleaning the dishes, we talked more about the cosmology of Daoism and the principles of meditation and qigong. "You'll learn more tomorrow," he said. We retired early to our thin cotton mats on the rustic wooden floor.

I awoke to the smell of fresh-baked bread and the sounds of the tropical woodlands. My host seemed eager for me to eat and get started on my walk. After breakfast, he accompanied me to the entrance of the long dirt road leading into the forest. "Just keep walking," he said. "It's all the way to the end." I joined my palms and bowed. He did the same.

After a few hours of walking, I came upon two men traveling in the opposite direction. They wore unique hats and were dressed similarly to my host. I deduced they must be Daoists. From quite a distance, I was struck by their Presence and the manner in which they walked. They seemed to move faster, lighter, and more fluidly than the average person. They appeared focused, yet not fixated. As we passed each other, they smiled at me but did not open their mouths or break their concentration. I stopped and watched. In that moment there was a silent transmission. I understood that walking held some unique power that I had not recognized before. For the rest of my journey, I tried to emulate the same spirit and fluidity. I noticed a different feeling in my body and spaciousness in my mind as I walked. It was as if I had learned something without learning it.

When I arrived at the end of the road, I felt rejuvenated and uplifted. There was an old weathered gate with a metal *Taiji* symbol in the center. I knew I was in the right spot. Nobody was around, so I set down my backpack, took out my journal, and began to write about my experience. After some time, a long-haired man approached from inside the gate. He was wearing loose-fitting black cotton pants and no shirt. He must have been over 50, but his body looked like that of a 20-year-old martial artist. His face was shining with a big smile. His long graying hair fell in waves over his shoulders.

We exchanged brief greetings. He seemed surprised and elated that I had come. There was a strange sense of familiarity, as if we had known each other for years. He cut right to the chase. "So, you want to learn?"

"Yes, very much so," I replied.

He smiled a little bigger. "Good, then stand up and try to hit me." At first I thought he was kidding.

He wasn't. I stood up and half-heartedly threw a punch that he easily avoided. "No, not like that. For real!" he said in a serious tone. I came at him with lefts and rights. He circled and moved gracefully, avoiding my strikes. "I'm an old man. You're a young man. What's the problem?" he said. We both cracked up laughing. I liked his light-hearted style.

We spent the next hour or so playing around, doing martial arts drills, handstands, and yoga poses. Each time he easily bested me. After we finished, he told me it was time to bathe before dinner. We walked into the jungle and followed the creek down a gorge to a beautiful waterfall. "There's your shower," he said. I was in heaven.

I stayed outside that gate for three days. Outsiders were not permitted inside the hermitage. During our short time together, he devoted every waking hour to teaching me. He taught me about diet, sexuality, meditation, and self-healing. He talked at length about the importance of saliva and preserving the Three Treasures.[15] I asked about the Daoists I had seen on the trail, if they were doing some special type of walking. He tapped his lower belly. "They walk from here," he told me. "*Dantien*![16] They walk with qi."

The central point he kept coming back to was that we must cultivate a virtuous energetic relationship with everything around us. He explained that all things are an expression of primordial energy (prana, qi), and that qi is the creative force of the divine. He taught me how to use qi to relate to plants, animals, and people; and how to feel the qi of Earth through my feet. "Whether walking, eating, or making love, we must be in good relationship with the qi," he exclaimed. "We have to be wholehearted in our actions."

On the third day, it was time for me to leave. He reiterated the main teachings we had discussed. "Never forget!" he implored. He gave me a big hug. We were both in tears. I put on my backpack, joined my hands to my heart, and bowed. It was hard for me to leave. Our connection felt timeless, it tugged at my very core. That was the last time I saw him. I spent the next 15 years digesting what I learned in those few days.

Key Points for Walking Practice
SPACE, FLUIDITY, PACE.
Space

Space in walking is maintained by cultivating a dynamic relationship with gravity and the vertical line. The feet touch the Earth with vibrant sensitivity, while the head floats upward to meet Heaven. There is a balance of downward rooting and upward lifting forces. Keeping a spacious, elongated feeling from head to feet allows the body to move and breathe with greater ease. Walking with awareness of inner space builds cushioning in the joints and facilitates the natural circulation of blood and vital energy through the whole body.

Fluidity

Fluidity occurs when body, breath, and mind function as one. During walking, we remain attentive to the tonus of our muscles, always working to stay relaxed and supple. This calms the nerves and fosters a smooth coordination of all the joints. By maintaining space and fluidity, a unique rhythm emerges—our Original Gait. As we walk, we blend with our environment, and our steps keep time with the pulse of life.

Pace

Pace is the specific speed we choose for a particular session of walking. There are two types of walking employed in the practice of the Four Dignities: Slow Mindful Walking and Walking Like the Wind. Slow Mindful Walking develops the ability to feel subtle nuances of our movement and breath pattern. Walking Like the Wind is a faster-paced stride that lets us appreciate the more dynamic aspect of fluid grace in motion.

Slow and fast-paced walking are equally valuable. The key is to work with pacing that feels genuine to you. The pace of your walking, whether slow, medium, or fast, should not feel forced or induce a feeling of mental or physical resistance. When first learning Slow Mindful Walking, it is not uncommon for the mind to become impatient. The habit of wanting to get somewhere may rear its head. This passes with continued practice.

Walking and the Vertical Axis

During the practice of walking and standing, the vertical axis runs through the longest measurement of the body: from head to feet. In walking, the body's relationship to the gravitational pull of the Earth is more dynamic than in the other three Dignities. We have forward motion, lateral rotation, the rise and fall of each step, and many other dynamics at play. Learning to feel the vertical axis while in motion is part of the fun.

Before you start each session of walking, take a moment to feel from the crown of the head down through the center of the body to the feet. Allow your body to organize around the vertical axis in such a way that the line of gravity runs through the center of the head, chest cavity, abdomen, and feet. Make subtle adjustments left, right, forward, and back, until you feel the greatest ease.

As you begin to walk, lean the vertical axis slightly forward. The degree of forward lean corresponds with pace. Momentum is gained with increased forward lean. Play around with the vertical axis while walking. Our purpose is not to walk fast per se, but to use the vertical axis as a tool to maintain whole-body feeling, somatic awareness.

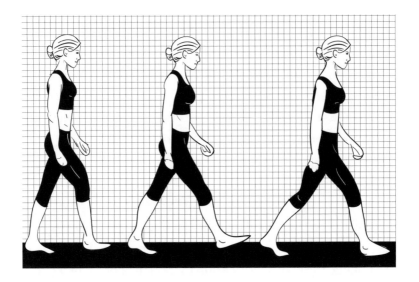

Dynamic Alignment of Walking
The Feet

FEEL THE EARTH.

Practicing barefoot gives the clearest response. Feel through the whole foot with each step. Take smaller strides, and maintain quiet, light heel strikes. It is helpful to think of the foot as having four corners: inner heel, outer heel, big toe, and little toe. Walk with the feet pointing forward so all four corners make contact with the floor. Steer the lower body from the hip joints, not the feet. This keeps a connection between the belly, hips, knees, and ankles, and allows the knees to hinge in their natural alignment.

The Knees

SHINE THEM FORWARD.

As you walk, point the kneecaps forward like two headlights. Adjust the feet to point straight ahead, by internally rotating the femurs just a little. The knees will find their smoothest hinge. Feel the knees gliding easy with each step.

The Hips

LET THEM MOVE.

It is essential to keep the hips soft and relaxed during walking. This comes from learning to feel. There are too many dynamics at play in the hips and pelvis to have a mental picture of what is happening during walking. To feel and let the hips flow is the key point.

The Chest

KEEP IT SOFT AND OPEN.

Holding the chest too far forward is overly ambitious and aggressive—the military posture. Collapsing the chest too far down is self-defeating and results in a reluctance to fully meet life. With each step, allow the chest to remain soft, neutral, and open. Finding the proper position gives a sense that the chest cavity is empty.

The Head

LET IT FLOAT.

Place one hand behind your head at the hairline. Gently press the head back into your hand while you brush the hand up the back of the head. This gives the feeling that the head is floating. The ears fall in the same line as the shoulders. As you discover the correct head position, it is important to keep the jaw and neck muscles relaxed. Remember, alignment is dynamic.

The Eyes

SEE EVERYTHING.

During walking practice, keep the eyes fully open and blink naturally. Do not let the eyes look here and there, or focus in on specific things around you. Rather, let the eyes rest in the sockets and point straight ahead. Let your vision be open and soft. Focus on nothing in particular. See everything.

"An early-morning walk is a blessing for the whole day."
Henry David Thoreau

Slow Mindful Walking

It is best to start your practice of walking with slow mindful movement. Working with slow walking for at least 100 days is the best way to build a solid foundation of embodied Presence during movement. Although we present two other types of walking practice here, Slow Mindful Waking is considered the essence of the practice of walking meditation.

Posture and Body Mechanics: In Slow Mindful Walking, forward lean is kept to bare minimum. Each step is taken with utmost care and sensitivity. Savor each part of the movement: the slow transition of weight from foot to foot, the peeling of the foot off the floor from heel to toe, and the setting down of the foot. From head to toe, keep the body relaxed and the movement natural. Step at a pace slow enough that you can feel each micro-movement.

Breathing: Allow the natural breath to extend out from the belly in all directions. The inhale ripples through the body, reaching the feet and head. Then, with the exhale, feel how the direction of breath moves back toward the belly. Let the shoulders settle down and the arms hang. Relax and let the unrestricted rhythm of your breathing animate your mindful motion.

Awareness: Feel Presence through the whole body. Keep your focus on the feeling of the body in motion. The mind may wander to thinking about other things. This is okay. Return to the sensation provided by slow walking. Keep coming back to fully participating in just walking. Become so fully present in the act of walking that everything else dissolves.

Duration: Start with a daily session of five minutes. Add one minute per week until you reach ten minutes. A ten-minute session is usually enough for most people to begin to get centered and drop in. Longer durations of walking will prove more powerful still. Continue adding one minute per week until you reach 20 minutes. There is a sweet spot that happens with a 20-minute session of Slow Mindful Walking. This is a good duration for general daily practice.

If you feel an inner pull to practice longer, attend to it. You can continue adding one minute a day up to 60 minutes and beyond. With longer sessions, remember to stay relaxed and be mindful of your posture. If any tension builds up, it might be a sign that you are overdoing it.

Unique Benefits: Walking cultivates heightened somatic awareness and harmony of body, mind, and breath. It strengthens focus, exposes and releases areas of chronic tension, develops strength of spirit, calms the nerves, improves balance, cultivates patience, and improves digestion.

Cautions: Remember, you are practicing stillness in motion. Although you are walking very slowly and maintaining a sense of inner stillness, do not hold the upper body rigidly motionless. This inhibits breathing and constricts the Vital Force. Also, do not let the hips jut forward, as this places strain on the lower back. Keep the head, torso, and hips in line with the vertical axis.

Walking Like the Wind

Walking at a brisk pace is a wonderful way to practice. In this method, we allow the forward motion to gather momentum and express its quickest natural pace. That is to say, we don't try to walk fast, yet we don't hold back either. The feeling is that we are being pushed forward by the wind. There is a sense of surrendering to a current of movement that is propelling us. We relax all effort and let ourselves move freely with nowhere to go. This is one of my favorite ways of expressing the Daoist axiom of "free and easy wandering."

This type of walking is best practiced in a larger space. For indoor walking, let the path of your motion meander anywhere it wants throughout the room. If you are practicing outdoors, head out on your walk with no particular destination in mind. Travel with nowhere to go. The quality of unpredictability is important in Walking Like the Wind. In the words of the *Dao De Jing*, "A good traveler has no fixed plans and is not intent on arriving." This is the spirit of Walking Like the Wind.

Posture and Body Mechanics: Since we are encouraging an increased pace, we need to allow our forward lean to intensify a little. As always, it is important to maintain good connectivity between the head, chest, and abdomen. The vertical axis is still intact, only now we lean into the movement a little and go! You can think of forward lean as the throttle of your walking. As you increase momentum, it is important to avoid trying to control the movement too much. The idea is to get out of the way and let the magic of total body coordination happen.

There is a natural harmony between the hips and shoulders that becomes more pronounced the faster you walk. The legs and arms both swing freely. This, along with the corresponding rotational dynamic of the spine, creates a powerful vector of movement. Increase momentum while reducing resistance. Walk like the wind.

Breathing: The increased speed of movement places a unique demand on the body for respiration. As always, there is no need to control the breath. Allow the whole body to breathe freely, with the belly as the Center. Keep the mouth closed and the face relaxed. This lets the nostrils adjust the temperature and humidity of the inhaled air. Appreciate how the breath changes with the practice of Walking Like the Wind compared with the more tempered expressions of the other Dignities.

Awareness: Feel the dynamic wholeness of your movement. Feel how the entire body coordinates around the Center of Being. Surrender the notion "I am walking by my own effort," and feel the more open qualities of Heaven, Earth, and Human cooperating to produce movement. Give yourself so fully to the act of walking that walking itself is all that remains.

Duration: Start with sessions of ten minutes, and built up from there. A daily practice of 20–30 minutes of Walking Like the Wind is perfect for people with a busy schedule. If you have more time, longer sessions are wonderful.

One way to deepen your practice is to take one day per month for personal retreat. On this day, experiment with a session of walking for several hours. It is important to be clear about your practice session. There is a different intent when practicing walking as opposed to just going for a stroll with friends. While practicing walking, just walk. Remain silent and inwardly aware.

Unique Benefits: Faster-paced walking is a fully fledged health tonic. It lightens the spirit and dissolves a thousand worries. It lubricates the joints and gives a rhythmic massage to the internal organs. It increases circulation of blood and vital energy, improves cardiovascular function, and relieves depression and anxiety. By allowing the arms to hang and swing rhythmically, the shoulders receive a much-needed massage. This softening of the shoulders allows the center of breathing to drop lower in the body. This is a key prerequisite for returning to Original Breath. Some yogic traditions say that this type of walking is the only daily exercise one needs to ensure longevity. As Hippocrates reportedly said, "Walking is a man's best medicine."

Cautions: Do not force yourself to walk fast. Don't hold back either. Be careful not to lead with the hips or chest too far forward. Move forward with the whole body as one, belly as Center.

Walking Backward

The practice of walking backward is a lesser-known method with many hidden benefits. It is said that walking backward takes us back in age, one step at a time, returning us to the unconditioned. Walking backward is an anti-aging tonic. This is to say that when we walk the opposite direction to usual, we can unwind learned patterns of perceiving and moving. Physically, the action of walking backward uses different muscles and requires a new kind of balance and coordination. This helps to reset the body. Because all of our main sensory organs are on the front of the head, walking backward develops a unique kind of awareness and immediacy.

Backward walking feels quite disorienting. This is part of it. Our whole system is confused by the unfamiliar biomechanics and different way of perceiving. This sets up a golden opportunity; we are free to experience a fresh sense of embodiment. The key is to keep walking amid the feeling of disorientation. A small dose of chaos gives way to a new kind of calm.

Walking backward is best employed if you are feeling stuck or having a difficult time physically, mentally, or emotionally. It is especially helpful if you are in serious pain, or if your mind is convincing you to skip your practice. It is one of the simplest and most effective ways of transforming obstacles into allies on the Path.

With all of the other practices in the Four Dignities, we outline key points of posture and body mechanics, breathing, awareness, duration, and so on. This helps deepen our understanding and clarify how to employ the different practices. However, with backward walking there is nothing of the sort to say. The whole point is to throw yourself into the raw strangeness of it, to abandon familiarity. It is a direct ticket to primal chaos (Chinese *huntun*). Just go for it. Walk backward with nowhere to go, no time to get there, and nothing at all to achieve. This is the spirit of walking backward.

Chapter 6

STANDING

"Do you believe there is some place that will make
 the soul less thirsty?
In that great absence you will find nothing.
Be strong then, and enter into your own body;
there you have a solid place for your feet.
Think about it carefully! Don't go off somewhere
 else!
Kabir says this: Just throw away all thoughts of
 imaginary things,
and stand firm in that which you are."

Kabir

The practice of standing is the most potent of the Four Dignities for strengthening the body and building up the Vital Force. It powerfully activates the thrive reflex and ignites the mysterious process of self-healing. It is also the most physically and mentally demanding. To stand still like a pine tree for 20 minutes a day is one of the best-kept secrets for health, longevity, and spiritual cultivation. The simple practice of standing still is a complete training tool for body, mind, and spirit.

There are countless positions and methods used for standing meditation. Methods are taught in different traditions for various purposes. In the Four Dignities practice, we use the two most essential positions. The first position is called the Wuji Position, or Empty Stance. The term Wuji refers to energy in its primordial, un-manifest form. The Empty Stance is the foundation of all other forms of standing meditation. The basis of this standing pose is to take our everyday way of standing and discover meditation within it. We simply stand with all the joints relaxed, arms hanging at the sides.

In this first posture, we are concerned only with naturalness. Keeping View and Method in collaboration, we practice a type of standing meditation that closely resembles "just standing." This is the spirit of the Wuji Position (see page 105 for illustration).

The second position is called Embracing the Tree, or Standing Pole. It expands on the principles employed in Wuji and adds a distinctive upper body and arm position that increases the energetic effects of the pose. In both positions, the lower body remains almost identical. The key feature of Embracing the Tree is the use of rounded upper body alignment. This teaches us how to centralize Presence and power in the lower belly, creating harmony between the upper and lower body. Learning to hold the arms up in a rounded shape, while keeping the shoulders and neck relaxed, is a challenging and rewarding process (see page 108 for illustration).

Discovering Standing Meditation

In 1998, I was living in Hawaii studying yoga and writing my first book. I was spending three to four hours a day practicing yoga postures, breathing exercises, and seated meditation. One afternoon, I went to Chinatown in Honolulu to shop for tea and herbs. I loved to visit the old herb shops with their timeless apothecary feel. The wall of small wooden drawers behind the glass display case of ginseng root and reishi mushroom held a charming mystique.

While waiting for the herbalist to package my herbs, I began talking with a Chinese man in the shop. He must have been around 40 years old. He had a stern-looking posture and notable Presence. I sensed he might be a martial artist. He asked me what I did. I told him I practiced and taught yoga. He asked me if I practiced meditation. I said, "Yes, it's the most important part of yoga practice." What he said next changed my view of meditation forever.

"Do you practice meditation standing up?"

I paused, slightly puzzled. "Uh, no, I practice sitting down. Why would I practice standing up?"

"Why would you practice sitting down?" he retorted.

I had never really thought about it. "Because I would imagine practicing meditation standing up is quite difficult," I said.

"Perhaps, but if you don't practice meditation standing up, you will never develop your true inner power."

Somehow I knew he was right. But I had never learned how to meditate standing up.

The herbalist slid my paper-wrapped bundle onto the glass display counter. My herbs were ready. My parking meter had probably already expired. It was time to pay and leave. I wanted to ask the man if he would teach me. I could feel that it was not the right time. "Thank you. I'm going to think more about what you said." The man remained silent, but his eyes spoke loud and clear: "Yeah, I bet you will."

I returned to my daily sessions of yoga and meditation. My practice was going well, but inside I felt something was missing. Something was nagging me from within. A few years later, I moved to Arizona to be near my ailing mother. While running errands one afternoon, I happened upon a small family acupuncture clinic in an unassuming strip mall. There was a paper flier on the door that read, "Qigong and Standing Meditation Class." A light bulb went off.

I showed up on the day of the class. The teacher was a middle-aged Chinese gentleman. His wife was working behind the desk and his kids were playing in the clinic. It felt more like a living room than a medical facility. I liked the warmth and casualness. Before class, the teacher handed me a glass bottle containing a formula of herbs. I looked at him, puzzled, wondering if he wanted me to take a sip. "Just unscrew the top," he said. I tried to unscrew the top but it didn't budge. I didn't want to force it, so I stopped and looked up at him. "Try the other way," he said. So I turned the top to the right and it unscrewed quite easily. He burst out laughing, "Some old Chinese herb bottles were threaded the opposite way." More laughter. "What you need to understand is that energy moves in circles and spirals. Using force is no good. Move *with* the spiral and everything is easy." My first lesson happened before class even started.

It was time for the class to begin. There were only a few students in attendance, all of us martial artists. The teacher had us arrange in a circle. "Now we practice Embracing the Tree." It was a crash course in standing meditation. He demonstrated the proper position: knees slightly bent, shoulders relaxed, arms round, as if embracing a large pine tree in front of you. He then came around and made corrections to our posture. Minutes went by. Five. Ten. Fifteen. Twenty.

Standing there seemed like an eternity. My shoulders tensed. My legs felt weak. My mind started to race. An onslaught of emotions flared up. "Relax and let the qi move freely through you," the teacher said. Something in me gave up. I stopped trying so hard. Without breaking the position, a kind of spaciousness opened inside me. Time seemed to disappear. The border between inside and outside seemed to blur. The circulation of my blood smoothed out. Breathing was effortless. There was a feeling of wholeness and radiance.

On that evening in Phoenix, I understood why the man from Honolulu was so adamant about standing meditation. From that day forward, I continued to study with many other teachers who helped refine my understanding of standing meditation. Through study and practice, I came to understand how standing is a powerful method of self-healing and spiritual cultivation.

Key Skills for Standing Practice
ROOTING, SOFTNESS, PATIENCE.
Rooting

Rooting is the quality of sinking your center of gravity lower in the body and making a tangible connection with the Earth. A tree is only as stable and healthy as its roots. So it is with a human being. In the practice of standing, rooting is the essential foundation upon which all other aspects of the practice depend. Rooting is subtle; it takes time to feel and understand. Our ability to root develops as we learn to feel through our whole body. With feeling, we discover how to relocate our awareness from the head to the heart to the belly. Like a stone sinking into water, we simply allow awareness to relax and descend into the Center of Being. There is a saying used in Chinese martial arts and qigong: "Sink the qi, lift the spirit." This implies dropping the sense of Presence and intensity into the belly, while cultivating a light-hearted and playful disposition.

Softness

Softness is the ability to keep the muscles and connective tissue in a state of relaxed poise. Think of the muscles of a cat. A cat can go from sleeping to running full speed in a split second. Cats are fast, agile, powerful, and resilient. This is because their bodies are free of tension. During standing practice, we work diligently to keep our body and mind free of tension. It is a two-part process. First, we must be able to identify tension. This requires increased somatic awareness. Second, we have to make an invitation for tension to release. The second part can be quite elusive. Often, as practitioners become more aware, they notice new areas of tension throughout the body. Yet they are unable to let this tension release. It is important to relate to tension in a respectful and gentle manner. Rejecting tension, or demanding that it go away, only makes it more intense. As the saying goes, "What you resist persists."

Softening is an action that must permeate the physical, mental, and emotional aspects of your being. This is what allows blood and Vital Force to circulate more freely through the whole body as you practice standing. Do not be discouraged if you find this difficult at first. With persistent practice, you will learn to soften.

Patience

Patience is the ability to remain spontaneously open to whatever the moment brings. Patience is intimate. Patience is courageous. Conventionally, patience is thought of as the capacity to wait for something. In the practice of the Four Dignities, we are never waiting for anything. We are one hundred percent engaged with *this* moment. Standing provides a wonderful test of patience. As one's patience grows, so too does inner strength. It is advised to first develop patience in the Wuji Position before advancing to Embracing the Tree.

Standing and the Vertical Axis

Of all the Four Dignities, standing gives us the most poignant feedback about our relationship with the vertical axis. If we are leaning even the slightest bit off the vertical line, our muscles will have to work extra hard to maintain the structure of standing. This places strain on the whole system, resulting in unnecessary tension and discomfort. It would seem that simply standing for 10–20 minutes should not be so challenging. Alas, it proves considerably more demanding than it appears. This is mostly due to subtle deviations from the vertical axis and constrictions in breathing. In other words, if our relationship to gravity is not optimal, our Original Posture and Original Breath will suffer.

As you practice standing, pay close attention to the feeling of the core of the body from head to feet. Make gentle micro-adjustments forward, back, left, and right until you find the most natural and relaxed vertical alignment. It is helpful to think of the head, chest, abdomen, and legs as four spheres floating one on top of the other. When these four are lined up, the whole body becomes one open space. The breath moves naturally, and blood and qi circulate freely. This invites a sense of relaxed poise.

Dynamic Alignment of Standing
The Feet
STUCK IN MUD.

A building is only as structurally sound as its foundation. The same is true of our body during standing. The feet are the essential foundation of our standing practice. It is not enough to feel that we are standing *on* the Earth. We need to feel as if we are standing *in* the Earth. Have the sense that your feet are buried in thick mud. This is a great help in rooting and stabilizing the whole body.

The Shins
VERTICAL LIKE THE BASE OF A TREE.

With the feet buried in mud, the shins serve like the base of a tree to create vertical stability for the whole body. Feel that the lower legs are strong and heavy. To keep the shins vertical, press the knees slightly apart. Then check to see that the outsides of the shins are perpendicular to the floor, and that the center of each kneecap is in line with the center of the foot. Don't press the knees out so far that they lose their alignment over the feet.

The Knees
ALIGNED OVER THE FEET.

Keep the knees unlocked. A slight bend in the knees lowers the center of gravity and allows the blood and qi to flow more smoothly. As the knees bend slightly, maintain the base established by the feet and shins by keeping the center of the kneecap in vertical line with the center of the foot.

The Thighs

MUSCLES RELAXED.

Consciously relax the upper legs. Maintain a feeling of suppleness in the front and back of the thighs. If the thigh muscles tense up, strain will be placed on the knees.

The Hips

SOFT AND FLUID.

Maintaining a neutral pelvis, keep the muscles around the hips feeling supple and fluid. This lets the power circulate between the lower and upper body, and provides a proper foundation for the entire spine.

The Lower Back

FILL IT UP.

"Fill up the lower back" is a saying I use to describe the feeling of anchoring the body's strength in the small of the back. You do this by maintaining a neutral pelvis while softening the fronts of the ribs down toward the belly.

Place the hands on the fronts of the lower ribs. Then slide your hands down toward your belly, feeling the ribs move down gently. This creates a lengthening and opening through the lower back. The breath can then move more freely in the ribcage and abdomen, which massages the lower back region. This subtle alignment is essential for maintaining a sense of comfort in the lower back, and developing connectivity between the upper and lower body.

The Upper Body

ROUND LIKE A BALL.

In both Wuji and Embracing the Tree, maintain a sense of roundness in the upper body. This means keeping all the joints unlocked and slightly curved. When the shoulders, elbows, wrists, and fingers all stay soft and supple, blood and qi circulate naturally and Original Breath happens by itself. In the beginning, you will have to constantly remind yourself to relax the muscles of the upper body and keep the feeling of roundness. With time, this becomes natural.

The Head

FLOATING LIKE A BUOY.

As you relax the upper body, the shoulders drop down away from the ears. This removes tension from the neck and frees the head. The head then floats upward like a buoy on water. You don't want to actively press the head up, as this will cause tension around the neck and jaw. Rather, find a sense of lightness in the head, coupled with the dropping of the shoulders. This allows the head to float upward by itself.

The Eyes

NOT OPEN, NOT CLOSED.

Let the eyes relax in the sockets. Allow the eyelids to close a little, but not all the way. Maintain at least a sliver of light in the eyes. This invites a sense of relaxed alertness.

The Standing Positions

There are two standing positions, each with a different orientation of the arms and upper body. In the Wuji Position, the arms hang at the sides. In Embracing the Tree, the arms are held up in front of the chest in a circular shape. The difference in arm position creates a distinctive alignment of the upper body, which causes subtle changes in breathing and energy flow. Embracing the Tree is considerably more challenging. It is advised to practice Wuji for at least 100 days before moving on to include Embracing the Tree.

Wuji Position: Empty Stance

Posture: Stand with the feet about one foot apart (use your foot to find the distance). To get the correct measurement for your body, place your right heel against the inner big toe joint of the left foot. The right foot is now perpendicular to the left. Then, keeping the ball of the foot on the floor, lift the right heel and rotate the right foot until it is parallel with the left. Your feet are now the proper distance apart for your body. Sometimes beginners find this width feels too narrow and perhaps uncomfortable. If this is the case for you, slightly increase the distance between the feet until you feel most comfortable. As your practice progresses, return to the original width and recheck the feeling.

Unlock the knees and soften the thighs. Fill up the lower back and feel spaciousness through the waist area. There is a sense that the ribcage is floating up above the hips. Soften the front of the ribs and the sternum. Let the arms hang at the sides with all the joints slightly bent. Then create a little space in the underarms as if holding a ping-pong ball in the armpit. This will cause the upper arm bones to move slightly away from the ribs, and allow blood to flow more freely to the arms and hands. Remember to keep the shoulders relaxed as you make this subtle adjustment. Keep the eyes horizontal and the nose vertical. Feel the interior of the body as one unified open space.

Breathing: Maintain natural breathing. Allow the breath to move freely through the whole body. Let the natural rhythm of breathing happen without restriction. Do not try to breathe deeply, but allow the breath to descend lower and lower into the body. Work only to remove any contrivance in the breath, and then let nature function.

Awareness: Let awareness descend to the soles of the feet. Keep your focus there for a while, feeling the descending quality of gravity. This will help settle the mind and relax the body. Then allow awareness to encompass the entire body. Remain with the totality of your direct embodied experience, moment by moment. Remember that awareness is open and luminous of itself. Let awareness remain just as-it-is.

Duration: Start by standing in Wuji for five minutes a day. Add one minute per week until you reach ten minutes. Stay with ten minutes for a few weeks to build up some steadiness. Then continue adding one minute per week again until you reach 20 minutes. A daily practice of 20 minutes is a good foundation.

After a year or more of practicing 20-minute sessions, if you are feeling pulled from within to stand for longer durations of time, you may continue slowly increasing week by week up to one hour. This is not a goal per se, but an honest answer to an inner calling.

Unique Benefits: The Wuji position teaches us how to relax while maintaining dynamic poise. The pose bolsters the flow of Vital Force in the bones, strengthens the legs and spine, activates the circulation of blood and qi, improves digestion, and harmonizes all the organ systems.

Cautions: Do not lock the knees. This can inhibit circulation and cause fainting. Do not bend the knees excessively, as this places undue strain on the knee joints.

Embracing the Tree

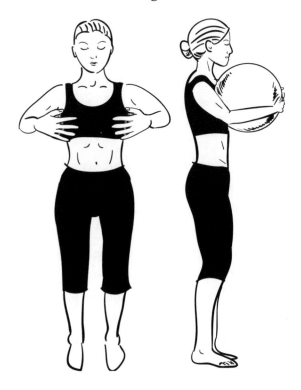

Posture: Stand with the feet about one foot apart (use your own foot to find the distance). To easily find this measurement, place your right heel against the inner big toe joint of the left foot. The right foot is now perpendicular to the left. Then, keeping the ball of the foot on the floor, lift the right heel and rotate the right foot until it is parallel with the left. Your feet are now the proper distance apart for your body. Maintain an equal balance of weight between the two feet. And maintain an equal balance of weight between the ball, arch, and center of the heel of each foot.

Sometimes beginners find this width feels too narrow and perhaps uncomfortable. If this is the case for you, slightly increase the distance between the feet until you feel most comfortable. As your practice progresses, return to the original width and recheck the feeling.

Unlock the knees and soften the thighs. Fill up the lower back and feel space through the waist area, as if the chest is floating up above the hips. Soften the front of the ribs and the chest. Then let the arms float up in front of the chest as if holding a large ball. Soften the shoulders and maintain the circular shape of the arms. Feel your arms squeezing in against the imaginary ball that touches the inner surfaces of the arms, palms of the hands, and chest. The tips of the fingers point toward each other, and the palms face your chest. The hands remain about 6–12 inches apart. Adjust the distance between the hands based on comfort. Relax the shoulders more, and feel as if the arms are floating. Keep the eyes horizontal and the nose vertical. Sense the central axis of the body aligned with gravity. Feel the center of gravity deep in the belly, somewhere below the navel.

Breathing: Allow the breath to sink lower into the belly and expand out to encompass the whole body. Feel the interior of the body as one open space and let the natural rhythm of the breathing happen without restriction. If the position gets physically or mentally challenging, do not attempt to breathe deeply. Simply invite tension to dissolve. Let the Vital Force wash through you with each breath cycle.

Awareness: Keep your heart-mind calm and serene. Feel the circular fluidity through every part of the body. Remain with the open and luminous quality of body and mind. Let this feeling-awareness permeate your being from skin to bone and from head to toe.

Duration: Embracing the Tree is the most physically challenging of all the Four Dignities positions. It is best to start with shorter duration and build up slowly over time. Begin practicing 2–5 minutes a day. For the first couple sessions, set a stopwatch to determine the amount of time it takes for you to feel any fatigue or discomfort in your shoulders. Use this as your base time. If the time is more than five minutes, use five minutes as your base.

It is essential to be honest with yourself and not skip ahead. Part of the discipline is to grow your practice little by little—slow and steady, like a tree. This builds a solid foundation. Add one minute every week to your base time until you reach a maximum of 20 minutes. A 20-minute daily practice of Embracing the Tree is excellent. It is best not to exceed 20 minutes without the guidance of a competent teacher to check the subtle nuances of your posture and breathing.

Unique Benefits: Embracing the Tree is a powerful cultivation practice. It improves the flow of energy in the whole body, strengthens the bones, muscles, tendons, and ligaments, and optimizes the function of all the organs. It develops mental and emotional stability, improves sleep, improves healing and martial power, and develops courage and perseverance.

Cautions: In the beginning, your shoulders will get easily fatigued. Do your best to relax and allow your lower body to do the work of holding your arms up. If you cannot relax, and the tension and discomfort in the shoulders is building up, it is time to take a rest. Slowly lower the arms, practice Walking Like the Wind for a few minutes, and then return to standing. It is good to challenge yourself, yet pushing through tension is not advantageous.

With the arms up, it is easy to lean the upper body back to compensate for the added forward weight. This is incorrect alignment and places strain on the spine. Have a partner check you from the side to make sure your whole body is remaining in line with the vertical axis.

Embracing the Tree is contraindicated during pregnancy.

Chapter 7

SITTING

"In the openness that arises spontaneously, free of all grasping, rest and relax, without contrivance or fabrication."

Longchenpa

Historically, the majority of contemplative traditions have strongly favored the seated position over all other positions used for meditation. It is easy to see why. The seated position offers stability, relative comfort, and a near perfect balance of poise and relaxation. The attentiveness necessary to maintain a naturally aligned sitting position keeps the mind alert. The relative ease most people experience while in the seated position allows for the possibility of a graceful transition from doing to Being. We are less likely to doze off in the seated position compared with the lying down positions. Conversely, it is easier to fall asleep while seated than while practicing standing or walking. As with all of the Four Dignities, each position has its stronger and weaker points. Cultivating all four is a powerful way to mitigate any potential weaknesses and maximize the virtues of our practice.

The Sanskrit word *asana* means "seat," and refers to the cushion a yogi sits upon to practice meditation. *Asana* also signifies any of the numerous bodily positions used in yogic practices. Yet the word *asana* implies much more than the shape and location of the body. A student once asked the great Indian sage Ramana Maharshi, "What is the best *asana*?" He replied, "Abidance in the Self is the only true posture." The Maharshi's loaded response hints at the importance of what we are calling embodied Presence. Remaining in our Original Nature is what matters most. If we strike an esoteric yoga position and lose our Original Breath and Original Posture, we have temporarily forfeited our Original Nature. Although such an *asana* may be technically correct and even display superior flexibility, balance, or strength, if we are not truly seated in our Center of Being, the pose is considered counter-productive in terms of spiritual cultivation.

We must apply the same thinking to our seated meditation position. If our seated position becomes forced—our spine ramrod straight, or our legs forced into full lotus with screaming knees—our practice will serve to strengthen the habit of ego-clinging. Sitting, as with all of the Four Dignities, must first and foremost be a natural expression. We start where we are. With daily practice, our posture, breathing, and mental state will go through various changes. Our hips will open, spine will find more freedom, and legs stop falling asleep as easily. It takes time. Our thoughts, emotions, and sensations will go through innumerable transformations as well. The point is to keep practicing.

The Spirit of Sitting

Seated meditation holds special significance in Asian spiritual art. For example, a statue of the historical Buddha seated in meditative equipoise evokes a certain resonance. There is recognition of some important aspect of ourselves. Something inside us says, "I want to feel like that. I want to be like that, so serene and collected." We intuitively know that we too have this Buddha-like quality. With continued practice of seated meditation, this subtle resonance pulls us ever inward toward the Center of Being. We discover Buddha is not a person, but our own intrinsic nature.

In traditions informed by the teachings of Laozi's *Dao De Jing*, the practice of simple sitting is referred to as *Zuowang* ("sitting and forgetting") or *Bao Yi* ("embrace one"). These names for the practice of non-conceptual seated meditation reflect back to the View behind our Method. "Sitting and forgetting" implies a kind of openness. When we sit, we forget our ambitions, we forget our personal preferences. We leave these things outside the practice space with our shoes. We embrace reality as-it-is and forget everything else. In terms of proper posture, as well as the spirit of seated meditation, we can learn much from the following passage by Suzuki Roshi: "When you sit you should settle yourself as if you were never going to stand up again." When we sit down to practice, we let go of conceptual toys to entertain the mind. We remain attentive to our posture and breath, moment by moment. This is the spirit of sitting.

Discovering Seated Meditation

At the age of 14, I joined a Japanese Cultural Center near my hometown. One of the main attractions of the center was the judo dojo. The center was steeped in tradition and the teachers in the dojo were kind and strict. For a teenage boy with too much energy, it was a perfect fit.

I remember my first day at the dojo as if it was yesterday. I had joined the wrestling team when I was 12 years old and had been training full-time for two years. I was lean and strong and felt pretty confident. Although I didn't know anything about judo, I figured my strength and wrestling skills would serve me well in the dojo. The *sensei* probably smelled my conceit as I walked in the door that day.

For the first round of *rondori* ("open practice"), he paired me with a Japanese girl who was at least a foot shorter than I was and weighed about 95 pounds. I thought to myself, "It's not fair to put her against me. She's just a little girl with a pony-tail." Little did I know she was one of the dojo's top students, and had been practicing judo since she could walk. *Sensei* yelled *Hajime!* ("begin"). Within ten seconds, I was flying through the air. I landed flat on my back on the cold firm mat. Disoriented and painfully humbled, I looked up to see my partner standing over me with a hint of a smile. In that moment, I understood first-hand that there was more to judo than strength and size. During that class, and many more to follow, I spent a lot of time flying through the air and hitting the mat.

Over the next few years, my peers and I spent hours practicing technique and strategy during weekly judo classes. We also learned many aspects of what might be called the warrior's code of conduct. Things like honor, discipline, humility, courage, and patience.

Zen historically influences the traditional Japanese arts: tea ceremony, brush calligraphy, swordsmanship, and flower arranging. The spirit of meditation is built into all of these. Judo is no exception. My first exposure to seated meditation happened on the judo mat. As part of our preparation for competition in weekend tournaments, our *sensei* taught us a simple form of meditation. At the end of class, he would have us sit quietly in *seiza* ("kneeling position") with our eyes closed. He would then instruct us to flawlessly perform our throws, arm bars, foot sweeps, and other techniques, using only our minds.

At first, I found this extremely difficult. I couldn't sit still or focus my mind for one minute. With repeated practice, however, I learned to visualize all of my judo techniques. I could see the subtle nuances of each move in slow motion or full speed. Not only did this new skill help me on the judo mat, the benefit spilled over into my schoolwork and other aspects of my life. Since that time in the dojo, seated meditation has continued to be the foundation of my personal practice.

The Vajra Seat

As we have said, form determines function. For our sitting to function as an expression of dignity and natural radiance, we have to refine our form. We have to work with our posture. This refinement of posture is not in the direction of a conceived notion of the "perfect posture." Refinement means remembering Original Posture. Refinement means dropping away conditioned patterns of tension and returning to the unconditioned.

Vajra is a Sanskrit word meaning "thunderbolt" and "diamond-like." It connotes the qualities of immediacy and incorruptibility. The Vajra Seat is a term used in yogic traditions to describe the potency of seated meditation. Such a power may be found with equal advantage on the floor or in a chair. The secret is to find a natural posture that expresses embodied Presence.

Let us look at the subtle details of the sitting postures, and discover tangible ways of cultivating the Vajra Seat.

Key Skills for Sitting Practice
BASE, COMFORT, POISE.
Base

Base is created through the parts of the body that touch the floor and/or chair. A solid and balanced base is the foundation of sitting practice. It is imperative that our base be firmly established; otherwise, the spine, upper back, and shoulders will tense up in an attempt to manufacture the stability that should be afforded by the lower body. Such a transition of stability from the lower to upper body causes constriction of the muscles around the abdomen and ribcage, which inhibits breathing and stresses the nervous system. Brute force of will and sheer muscular effort are of no use in the practice of sitting. Original Posture and Original Breath depend on true base. This means that the lower body forms the base and the belly is the center of gravity. It happens by surrendering to the downward force. The upward force happens automatically when we cultivate base and allow the upper body to relax and float.

We will address the details of how to create base while seated on the floor as opposed to in a chair in the sections on dynamic alignment below.

Comfort

Comfort arises from the ability to face yourself. Finding comfort in sitting takes patience and a willingness to experiment and explore our own physiology. The comfort we are going for here is not the type of indulgent comfort we find while slouching on a sofa. Good sitting posture includes a natural sense of ease without losing our majesty and Presence. It is important to understand that comfort does not mean feeling exclusively pleasant sensations. Comfort in sitting is as much a matter of spiritual contentment and natural breathing as it is physical sensation. True comfort is available amid experiences we deem pleasant, unpleasant, or neutral. Comfort comes from an underlying sense of intimacy with things, knowing that everything is okay as-it-is.

Poise

Poise is the sense of being upright and candid. Physically, our spine must have poise or our sitting practice will collapse into dullness. Spiritually, we cultivate a sense of immediacy. In this way, our sitting becomes genuine and fresh. It has the quality of timelessness. When we sit, our objective is to sit honestly. It seems obvious, yet there is a strong temptation to use spiritual practice as a means of avoiding our actual situation. Poise is the sense of being fully where we are. This can be seen in our posture and heard in our breathing. Poise is both a tool for practice and the fruition of practice. It is an important part of cultivating Original Posture, Original Breath, and Original Nature.

Sitting and the Vertical Axis

During the practice of sitting, the vertical axis is the shortest of the three upright Dignities. In walking and standing, the axis runs the full length of the body from head to feet. In lying down, the axis runs perpendicular to the spine. In sitting, the axis stretches from the top of the head to the seat. In a sense, this makes the work of aligning with the vertical line a bit easier. There is less area to cover. In sitting, if our base is well established, the vertical line practically adjusts itself.

Nevertheless, we still need to be attentive to the position of the three main spheres of the body: head, chest, and belly. Feel the imaginary line running through the center of the head, neck, chest cavity, and belly. By keeping the center point of the crown of the head in vertical line with the center point of the pelvic floor, the rest of your body will naturally organize around the axis. It is important to remember that this alignment is dynamic.

There is movement in stillness. We don't want to feel stacked up and rigid, like a pile of books.

The act of being attentive to the vertical axis is one of the simplest and most powerful ways of cultivating embodied Presence during sitting. It is also serves to connect us more fully with the current of vital energy flowing between Heaven and Earth. When we remain aligned with the vertical axis, the healing power of nature operates with greater potency within us.

Dynamic Alignment of Sitting
The Feet
ASSIST THE BASE.

While practicing seated meditation in a chair, the feet and sitting bones form the base. The feet must be flat on the floor and solid, as if you were about to stand up. While seated on the floor, the sitting bones form the primary base, while the legs and feet assist, to a greater or lesser degree, depending on the position. In both cases, it is important to feel the feet and their role in creating base.

The Sitting Bones
EQUAL LEFT AND RIGHT.

In all seated positions, the sitting bones form the main structure of the base. It is imperative that your weight be distributed equally through the left and right sitting bones. This balances the spine and helps establish the vertical axis. It is also helpful to shift the weight slightly forward on the sitting bones. This reduces the tendency to place pressure on the sciatic nerve, which can increase the likelihood of the legs falling asleep. A slight shift forward on the sitting bones also supports the natural lumbar curve.

The Hip Creases

HIGHER THAN THE KNEES.

This is the single most important alignment rule to remember when practicing seated meditation. The fronts of the hips, where the tops of thighs meet the pelvis, must be higher than the knees. This supports the natural curve of the lower back, and allows the muscles around the legs and hips to relax. This is essential for cultivating Original Posture and Original Breath. If the knees are higher than the hips, the belly will compress and the lower back will bulge backward, reversing the natural curve of the lumbar spine.

Use a meditation cushion, blanket, or bolster to elevate the sitting bones as high as you need to get the knees lower than the hip creases. The height difference between the hips and knees doesn't need to be excessive. Just a little will do—enough that if you were to pour water on your upper thigh, it would flow toward your knee.

The Belly

OPEN AND RELAXED.

It is important to avoid compressing the belly while we practice sitting. To keep the belly open and relaxed, the hips need to be higher than the knees. Then the belly will have space to expand and contract as the diaphragm moves with each breath. In seated meditation, and in all activities, feel the belly as the Center of Presence.

The Spine
TALL AND FREE.

Maintain length from the tailbone to the crown of the head. This reduces compression on the spinal disks, and maintains a cushion of space between each vertebra. Feel your spine is luminous and spacious.

The Shoulders
MELTING DOWN.

As with all of the Four Dignities, we want to keep the shoulders relaxed and settled. Feel the shoulders effortlessly drop, like a silk cape falling down your back. Avoid pressing the shoulders down muscularly, as this causes tension and inhibits the natural motion of breathing.

The Hands
GENTLY RESTING.

The hands may rest on the thighs with the palms facing down, or against the lower belly, with the palms touching the belly. These two positions are balanced and grounding. Although popular, it is not advised to practice with the hands on the thighs, palms facing up. This can encourage a sense of disembodiment and spaciness.

The Head
EMPTY.

"Empty the head" implies a movement from thinking to Being. We can simply let the fullness of the head descend into the ocean of the belly, like a stone sinking into deep water. This reduces the tendency to be top-heavy and self-conscious. It also lowers the center of gravity and connects us with the source of primal energy

(*Shakti*). There is a sense of having the Sun in the belly, and the cool night Sky in the head.

The Eyes

HORIZONTAL.

Let the eyes rest in the sockets, pointing forward. If we look too far down, we will become drowsy. If we look too far up, it's easy to get excited. With the eyes horizontal, let seeing rest in open space, one arm's length in front of you. Allow the eyes to be both open and closed. This means the eyes are not fully open or intentionally closed, but somewhere in between. It is difficult to say how open the eyes should be. This is for each of us to discover. At least a sliver of light can be seen.

Many students report that finding the natural position of the eyes is one of the most challenging aspects of sitting. Be patient. Be persistent. If keeping the eyes slightly open causes significant strain or discomfort, practice with closed eyes for a while. Revisit the slightly open eye position once other aspects of your practice have stabilized.

How Long to Sit

The following recommendations on duration apply to all the seated meditation positions listed below. Start with sessions of ten minutes per day of seated meditation, and add one minute per week until you reach 20 minutes. A daily practice of 20 minutes is good for most people. You can stay with 20 minutes for as long as you like.

Once you have established a consistent practice of 20 minutes per day for at least 100 days, you can again start adding one minute per week until you reach 30 minutes. Once more, commit to 100 days of 30 minutes a day of sitting. Then add one minute per week until you reach 40 minutes. Commit to 100 days of 40 minutes a day. Continue using this same time schedule to build up from 40 minutes to 50 minutes to one hour of sitting per day. If you miss a day during any of your 100-day committed practice periods, start over with that 100-day set. This keeps your discipline honest and your heart true. Building up slowly will ensure that your personal practice is genuine. There is no rush to get anywhere. Don't push forward. Don't hold back either. If fear of sitting longer is deterring you, confront it. If laziness gets in your way, conquer it. If professional or personal commitments truly limit the amount of time you can practice, do not despair. Respect your situation, and do your best.

As with all the Four Dignities, there is no perfect duration or specific goal to reach for sitting. If your natural appetite is interested in exploring meditation deeper, you will probably desire to spend more time with the Dignities. If this is the case for you, following a structured practice schedule is crucial in avoiding common obstacles such as inconsistency, laziness, doubt, and excess ambition. When you reach a duration that feels adequate for you, stay with that for some months or years. If you have the opportunity to attend group practice sessions or an intensive practice retreat, these will help strengthen your personal practice considerably.

Sitting on the Floor

There are two basic ways of creating base while sitting on the floor: the cross-legged position and the kneeling position. There are many variations of these two styles of sitting. The dynamics of how each position creates base can be divided into two main categories. Cross-legged positions use the sitting bones, buttocks, outer thighs, shins, ankles, and feet as contact points with the floor. In any variation of cross-legged sitting, a combination of these points will touch the floor, bear weight, and create base. This creates a wide and stable foundation.

In any variation of the kneeling position, the knees, front of the shins, tops of the ankles, and feet touch the floor. The sitting bones rest on the heels, a bench, or a cushion. This combination of contact points bears weight and creates base in the kneeling positions. For all of the floor positions, it is advised to sit upon a padded surface, instead of directly on the floor. A yoga mat, folded blanket, or traditional Japanese *zabuton* (cotton mat) all work well.

Cross-Legged Positions

There are five cross-legged positions outlined below. The main difference between the positions is the arrangement of the legs, and the need for props in supporting the sitting bones and/or knees. Two of the cross-legged positions are symmetrical and three are asymmetrical. This affects the distribution of weight through the sitting bones, and thus the alignment of the spine. Easy Pose and Full Lotus are considered symmetrical. Half Lotus, Quarter Lotus, and the Burmese Position are considered asymmetrical. Each position has its strengths and weaknesses. When exploring the positions, choose the one that feels most natural and provides the best combination of comfort and stability for your body.

Easy Pose

Easy Pose is the basic cross-legged floor position. It is the yoga position called *Sukhasana* (Sanskrit "pleasant pose"). Easy Pose is the simplest of the seated poses and requires the least flexibility in the hips. However, to ensure that the hips are above the knees, you may need a few props.

Posture: First, use a meditation cushion or stack of blankets tall enough so that the hip creases rest higher than the knees. Once you establish this height, the knees will be floating in space and no longer contributing to the base. This places pressure on the ankles and will irritate the muscles of the inner thighs over time. To mitigate this potential misalignment, place a firm cushion under each knee. You can use a foam yoga block or pillow. This provides downward stability through the knee into the floor. You may have to experiment with different props to find the right combination that best supports your lower body.

Once the lower body base is established, the upper body can relax and float. Elongate the spine and let the shoulders soften down away from the ears. Feel the arms hanging from the shoulders. Rest the hands on the thighs, palms facing down. Feel the chest open and soft, and the lower ribs descend into the belly. Lightly press the back of your neck into your shirt collar, and extend up through the crown of the head.

Breathing: Surrender and let the Great Respiration happen unimpeded. Soften the body from head to toe and let the natural movement of your breathing ripple through every part of the body.

Awareness: Moment by moment, remain with felt-awareness through the whole body. Feel the interior of the body as one hollow space, with your belly as the Center.

Unique Benefits: Easy Pose is perhaps the best place to start for beginners wanting to practice seated meditation on the floor. It does not require exceptional flexibility in the hips, and can be easily supported with a wide range of props to assist comfort.

Cautions: If your hips are tight, you will need to elevate your sitting bones considerably higher than you might think to achieve the proper hip-to-knee relationship. As your meditation seat gets taller, there is an increased risk of losing stability. Take the extra time to make sure your seat is stable and that your knees are properly supported.

Burmese Position

The Burmese Position uses a split-legged arrangement, where one leg is next to the body and the other rests in front of the inner leg. This provides a wide and stable base. It requires a little more flexibility in the hips compared with Easy Pose, yet considerably less than any of the Lotus variations. Because the two legs are in slightly different relationships to the torso, the pose is uneven. The unevenness of the legs causes a small tilt of the pelvis left or right, depending on which leg is forward. So, if you use the Burmese Position, it is important to alternate which leg is in front with each practice session. This protects you from developing structural imbalance.

Posture: As always, we want the hip creases to be higher than the knees. This is more easily accomplished in the Burmese Position than in Easy Pose. A basic meditation cushion usually provides enough height. However, some people find they need a little extra lift to get the knee-to-hip relationship just right. If this is the case for you, place a folded blanket under your meditation cushion for a little extra height.

Once the lower body is in position, feel the spine long and the head floating up like a helium balloon. Let the shoulders settle down and the arms hang. Rest the hands on the tops of the thighs, palms facing down. Keeping the eyes horizontal and the nose vertical, draw the chin slightly in toward the throat.

Breathing: Soften the body from skin to bone and let Original Breath function. Feel the natural ebb and flow of breathing happen by itself. Resist the temptation to assist the breath. Let the Vital Force breathe through you.

Awareness: Anchor yourself in immediate Presence. Rest in the Center of Being and let all things take their course. Do not stand aloof, but let the clear light of awareness warmly embrace all things exactly as-they-are.

Unique Benefits: The Burmese Position is used in esoteric yoga traditions to help sublimate sexual energy. The operative factor here is the foot placed closest to the body, which exerts gentle pressure on the opening of the genitals, effectively "sealing" sexual energy inside the body.

Cautions: For some people, the split-leg position causes minor torsion on the front knee. This sensation may not arise until 10–20 minutes into a session of sitting. If this is the case for you, try placing a thin pillow under the front knee. This usually changes the angle enough to eliminate the problem. Remember to alternate legs with each practice session.

Quarter Lotus

Quarter Lotus is similar to the Burmese Position, except the lower legs are stacked instead of one in front of the other. This brings the shinbones onto the same plane, which some people find more comfortable than the staggered shin arrangement in the Burmese Position. Quarter Lotus is asymmetrical, so it is important to switch which leg is on top with each practice session to avoid creating an imbalance.

Posture: Start by sitting on your meditation cushion in Easy Pose. Draw the lower foot as close to your pubic bone as you comfortably can. Then place the top foot on the inner calf of the lower leg, in the crease between the lower calf and thigh. Experiment with the location of the upper foot until you find the most comfortable position. At this point, the top knee is usually off the floor. Use a folded blanket, foam yoga block, or pillow under the knee for support.

With the lower body as a firm base, the upper body can soften and effortlessly fall into alignment. Allow the head to float upward, elongating the spine. Let the shoulders settle and the arms hang. Rest the palms on the tops of the thighs. Slide the head back, so that you feel the vertical axis running through the head, chest, and belly.

Breathing: Empty yourself of concepts and let the Great Respiration happen through you. Remain attentive to your breathing, but do not attempt to breathe in a specific way. If you notice areas of tension or fixation, invite these to soften, so that the primordial energy may move freely through you.

Awareness: Innate wakefulness is complete of-itself. There is nothing you need to *do* to produce this. Simply relax and take refuge in non-discriminatory awareness.

Unique Benefits: Although Quarter Lotus is a solid pose in its own right, it can also serve as a good stepping stone for people wishing to open their hips enough to practice Half Lotus or Full Lotus. With time, as the breath and Vital Force move more freely through the body, many people find that their hips become more supple, and that poses requiring greater range of motion become comfortable.

Cautions: With one leg resting on top of the other, there is an increased likelihood that the lower leg will fall asleep. This is due to a constriction of blood flow produced by the weight of the top leg pressing downward. Explore subtle adjustments in the location of the top leg until you find the best position. Remember to alternate legs each practice session.

Half Lotus

Half Lotus is similar to Quarter Lotus. The difference is that one foot rests on top of the opposite thigh. This requires considerably more flexibility and range of motion in the hips. Some people find Half Lotus creates a firmer base and a greater sense of stability. When working with Half Lotus, it is important that you pay closer attention to the feeling in your knees. At no time should you feel pressure or discomfort in the knee joints. This is a sign that the hips are not ready for the pose, and that the knee joints are in torsion. Forcing the Half Lotus pose can result in knee damage over time. Respect your body and work gently.

Posture: Start sitting on your meditation cushion in Easy Pose. Draw the lower foot as close to your pubic bone as you comfortably can. Then place the top foot on the opposite thigh close to the hip crease. Allow the toes to extend slightly beyond the thigh. Lightly flex the toes back toward the top of the foot. This protects the knee. Experiment with the location of the upper foot until you find the most comfortable position. At this point, the top knee is usually off the floor. Use a folded blanket, foam yoga block, or pillow under the knee for support.

Half Lotus is asymmetrical; therefore the alignment of the pelvis will not be perfectly level. Change which foot you place on top with each practice session to avoid structural imbalance.

Allow the lower body to be heavy and the upper body light. Maintain length in the spine, and feel the head, ribcage, and belly all in line with the vertical axis.

Breathing: Let the Vital Force move freely through the unified open space of the body. From skin to bone, let Original Breath follow its own rhythm.

Awareness: Stay anchored in the self-existing ground of Being that precedes intent and conceptualization. Take refuge in the open quality of clear light Presence.

Unique Benefits: Half Lotus creates a locking mechanism with the top foot that provides a unique feeling of solidity. Some people find that this sense of being partially locked into the posture helps them more easily feel the quality of immediate Presence.

Cautions: As mentioned above, Half Lotus can be hard on the knees if the hips are not open enough and the body is not ready. Do not let ambition or "spiritual ego" drive you to sit in this pose before your body is honestly ready.

Full Lotus

Full Lotus is considered the perfect pose for seated meditation. It creates a solid symmetrical base that supports the upright spine in an exceptional way. However, the pose requires extraordinary flexibility and range of motion in the hips. For most people who did not grow up sitting cross-legged on the floor, performing Lotus Pose correctly can take years of preparation. The connective tissue around the hips must be slowly conditioned in such a way that the pose does not place strain on the knees. Some people may not be able to perform Lotus Pose properly, even after decades of yoga practice. This is usually due to skeletal restrictions of the hip sockets and femur bones, not tight muscles or fascia.

Once the base is established, the upper body can relax and open. Feel the spine elongate from the tailbone to the crown of the head. Let the shoulders melt down away from the ears. Rest the hands on the tops of the thighs, palms down. Move the head slightly back to maintain the vertical axis.

Full Lotus is a powerful pose and it must be respected. Performed correctly, it can be a wonderful aid to seated meditation practice. When forced or practiced incorrectly, it can cause serious damage to the knees, hips, and ankles. If you are working toward sitting in Full Lotus, or if you can already perform the pose correctly, it is best to start with shorter sessions of sitting and work up slowly to 20 minutes or more.

Posture: Start by sitting on the floor in Easy Pose. Draw the right foot as close to your pubic bone as you comfortably can. Place your hand on the inner right thigh and rotate the flesh outward toward the floor. Continue externally rotating the right thigh as you gently bring the right foot onto the left thigh. Then place your hand on the inner left thigh and rotate the flesh outward toward the floor. Continue externally rotating the left thigh as you gently bring the left foot onto the right thigh. Pay attention to the feeling in your knees. If there is any sensation of discomfort in the knees, come out of the pose. If the knees feel good, use your hands to gently pull the feet up the thighs toward the hip creases. Allow the toes to extend slightly beyond the thighs. Lightly flex the toes back toward the top of the foot. This protects the knees and locks the pose in place.

Experiment with the location of the feet until you find the most comfortable position. At this point, the top knee may be slightly off the floor. If that is the case, use a folded blanket or thin pillow under the knee for support. Even though Lotus Pose is relatively symmetrical, it is good to alternate which foot is on top with each practice session. This helps maintain energetic and structural balance.

With the lower body locked into place, the upper body alignment almost happens by itself. Nevertheless, run through the checklist: spine long, shoulders down, chest open, arms hanging, hands resting on the thighs, chin drawn slightly in, eyes horizontal.

Breathing: Allow the natural rhythm of your breathing to happen by itself. Notice how the incoming breath originates at the belly, and how the outgoing breath returns to the belly. Relax and feel the body and universe breathing as one.

Awareness: Remain completely attentive to the immediate moment. Release all interest in personal gain. Relate to each moment candidly. Simply stay within Original Posture, Original Breath, and Original Nature.

Unique Benefits: Lotus Pose is a whole-body mudra, an energetic seal. It sets up a unique flow of energy in the body that perfectly supports upright posture and mental clarity. It is also one of the only postures that does not require the use of a meditation cushion, although many people find the pose more comfortable when the sitting bones are slightly elevated.

Cautions: Lotus Pose is an exhilarating position. Even though you are moving into the pose gently, it is easy to get over-zealous and ignore subtle warning signs from the body. We must approach the pose with humility and honesty; in other words, keep ego in check. Pay close attention to your joints, especially the knees, and come out of the pose at the first sign of any discomfort in or around your joints.

Kneeling Positions

Historically, the kneeling position has been used most commonly in Japan, where it is referred to as *seiza* (Japanese "sitting correctly"). Kneeling on the floor is usually done on *tatami* mats, and is the preferred sitting position in martial arts, calligraphy, and tea ceremony. In traditional Japanese culture, there are subtle nuances to *seiza* depending on the context and what one is wearing. There are also differences in the way men and women sit in *seiza*. Within the environment of traditional Japanese arts, it is important to understand the nuances of *seiza*.

However, for the purpose of meditation, we are mainly concerned with comfort and stability. And, for many people, the kneeling position provides both of these. Sitting meditation in the kneeling position may be practiced three different ways: kneeling on the floor, kneeling with a cushion under the sitting bones, or kneeling on a specially made meditation bench.

Seiza: Floor-Kneeling

Posture: Come to the floor in a kneeling position with the sitting bones resting on the heels. Separate the knees to the width that feels most comfortable to you. The tops of the feet and toenails are rooted into the floor. Remember to use a folded blanket or yoga mat as padding for the knees and shins. This lower body position creates a firm base and usually encourages neutral pelvic alignment and natural lumbar curve. However, it is still important to fine-tune these two points of alignment for your body.

Once you feel the pelvis and lower back are in good position, align the ribcage directly over the hips. Allow the lower ribs to melt down toward the belly. Soften the shoulders and place the palms of the hands on the tops of the thighs. Draw the chin slightly back, and extend upward through the crown of the head.

Breathing: *Seiza* automatically encourages full-body breathing. Remaining centered in the belly, simply allow this to happen by itself. Soften any areas of tension that you feel inhibit the movement of Original Breath.

Awareness: Feel the heaviness of the lower body (Earth) and the lightness of the upper body (Heaven). Remain centered in clear light awareness.

Unique Benefits: *Seiza*, practiced without a meditation bench, has an especially powerful healing effect on the digestive system and lower back. This is due to the pressure placed on the legs, which increases blood circulation to the abdomen. The pose is grounding and centering; it reduces anxiety, increases willpower and confidence, and bolsters the Vital Force.

Cautions: The kneeling position, done without a meditation bench, can be challenging on the knees and ankles. As always, honor your body. Hold the position for shorter periods at first, and then build up slowly over time. If there is any acute discomfort in the knees or ankles, come out of the position. If you cannot comfortably sit *seiza* directly on the floor, you may find it helpful to place a firm cushion under your sitting bones, between your legs. This significantly reduces pressure on the knees and ankles.

Kneeling on a Meditation Bench

Posture: Kneeling on a meditation bench is essentially the same position as *seiza*. The difference is that the bench, instead of your legs, supports the majority of your body weight. Even though there is less pressure on the knees and shins, it is still best to use a folded blanket or yoga mat under your legs as padding.

Kneel on the floor with the bench to your side. Lift the sitting bones away from your heels and place the bench over your lower legs. Your lower legs remain on the inside of the vertical supports of the bench. With the tops of the feet flat on the floor, lower your sitting bones onto the seat of the bench. Separate the knees until you find the most comfortable width. Then adjust the position of your pelvis and lower back to find neutral alignment. The lower body base is now established.

Lengthen the space between your hips and ribs. Then let the fronts of the ribs melt down toward the belly. Gently open the chest and broaden across the collarbones. Let the shoulders sink down away from the ears. Rest the palms of the hands on the tops of the thighs. Draw the chin in slightly, and float the head toward Heaven.

Breathing: Allow the breath to sink down into the lower belly. Do not willfully force the breath down or press the belly out. Instead, feel that the breath is being drawn by the belly. The air enters through the nostrils, travels through the throat, chest, solar plexus, and down into the belly. It exits in the reverse. Remain with the feeling of spontaneous natural breathing.

Awareness: Awareness is innately luminous and warm. It accepts all manifestations as-they-are. Go directly to that open dimension of awareness. Remain with the felt-sense of body and the potency of clear light Presence.

Unique Benefits: Using a meditation bench can be revolutionary for those who prefer the kneeling position but cannot tolerate sitting directly on the heels. Even with knee injuries or arthritic conditions, many people find this supported position comfortable. If none of the cross-legged positions prove acceptable, using a meditation bench may be the answer.

Cautions: Always use padding under the knees and shins when practicing the kneeling position, even with a bench. You may need more padding than you initially realize. Try folding a yoga mat in half, then placing a blanket on top of that. If you have longer legs, you may need to use two yoga mats, one on top of the other, covered by a blanket.

Maitreyasana: Chair-Sitting Posture

For people who did not grow up in a culture that frequently sits on the floor, using a chair for meditation might be superior. Years of struggling to find a comfortable position on the floor can become an unnecessary obstacle to meditation practice. In Buddhist iconography, the posture of sitting in a chair for meditation is called *Maitreyasana*. Maitreya is a bodhisattva, mentioned in the Pali Canon, who is believed to be the successor of the historical Buddha Shakyamuni. Many believe Maitreya is a world teacher who appears on Earth to show the Way during a modern era where ignorance and spiritual poverty are commonplace. Sometimes referred to as the "Buddha of our time," Maitreya is often depicted sitting in a chair with his feet on the ground.

We have all seen countless images of buddhas and yogis sitting cross-legged on lotus flowers or under majestic trees. These images are indeed heart-stirring. Yet the notion that cross-legged sitting is imperative for spiritual cultivation must be challenged. After 20 years of yoga and meditation practice, I am thoroughly convinced that sitting in a chair is only inferior to sitting on the floor in one way: it requires the use of a chair. With cross-legged or kneeling postures, you can practice anywhere, even in the forest.

However, times have changed. Most people live in urban or suburban areas where sitting on the floor might be more cumbersome than finding a chair. For many modern people, not only has the body become unaccustomed to floor sitting, but our houses and buildings are usually not set up with floor seating in mind. For example, it is not advised to sit on the floor in a room with tall furniture, electronics, or high windows. For these reasons and more, practicing seated meditation in a chair will be the best choice for many people.

Posture: Find a stable chair, preferably made of natural materials. It is important that the chair feels solid and does not wobble. Sit down on the chair with your sitting bones toward the front of the seat. Place your feet flat on the floor. Make an assessment of the height of your knees in relation to your hips. If the hip creases are higher than the tops of the knees, the chair is a good height for you. If not, you will need to place some padding under your sitting bones to achieve the right alignment. You can use a sturdy pillow or a folded blanket to adjust your height as needed.

Once you achieve the proper hip-to-knee alignment, you are ready to build the four-pointed base of *Maitreyasana*. Creating base while seated in a chair is quite different from on the floor, yet just as essential. With your sitting bones just a few inches from the edge of the seat, you will not be using the back of the chair during seated meditation, unless you have a health condition that requires the use of a backrest. Rock slightly forward on the sitting bones, so that your tailbone does not touch the chair. This sets the pelvis in a neutral position and preserves the lumbar curve. Separate the feet shoulder-width apart, with the toes pointing straight ahead. Make sure the shins are vertical, and that the knees are directly above the feet. The feet must bear weight and be energized, as if you were about to stand up and walk briskly.

Get set in your position, then stand up quickly a few times. This will help you understand the true spirit of sitting in a chair. The posture and attitude are rooted yet light; you are ready to stand up at any time.

The two feet and two sitting bones form the four-pointed base of *Maitreyasana*. Feel that each of the four points carries 25 percent of your body weight. In reality, the sitting bones will bear more weight than the feet. Yet feeling that the feet carry more weight will increase the solidity of your base and take excess pressure off the sitting bones.

With the lower body in good form, the upper body position is basically the same as with the other seated postures. Feel the spine elongate from the tail to the crown. Draw the head slightly back so it rests in line with the ribcage and abdomen, in line with the vertical axis. Let the shoulders descend away from the ears, and the arms hang free from the shoulder sockets. Place the hands on the thighs, palms facing down.

Breathing: From the bottoms of the feet to the top of the head, feel the movement of the breath rippling through the body. Feel that your body fills the space between Heaven and Earth, and the natural ebb and flow of the Vital Force has space to move within.

Awareness: Relax and appreciate the spirit of uninterrupted spontaneous acceptance. No matter what arises within your experience, let it take its own course. Thoughts, sensations, emotions—know that all things are self-resolving. Take refuge in the self-originating clear light of awareness.

Unique Benefits: Practicing seated meditation using the Chair-Sitting Posture is exceptionally balanced. It is particularly useful for people who cannot comfortably sit on the floor or do not have a place in their home where floor-sitting makes sense. The posture and Presence cultivated during chair-sitting easily spills over into every other aspect of modern life: dining, driving, studying, sitting on busses or planes, and so on.

Cautions: Be mindful not to let your tailbone touch the seat of the chair. This slight shift of the pelvis causes compression of the spinal column, reverses the lumbar curve, and inhibits the natural flow of cerebrospinal fluid and Vital Force.

Chapter 8

LYING DOWN

"By remaining motionless for some time and keeping the mind still while you are fully conscious, you learn to relax. This conscious relaxation invigorates and refreshes both body and mind."

B. K. S. Iyengar

There is a common saying among yoga practitioners, "*Savasana* is the easiest hardest pose." The word *Savasana* derives from the Sanskrit roots *sava* meaning "corpse" and *asana* meaning "pose" or "seat." *Savasana* is the final resting pose usually performed at the end of a series of yoga postures. The easy part of practicing *Savasana* is that all you have to do is lie down and relax. Sounds simple enough. Yet anyone who has been to a yoga class knows full well the hidden challenges this pose presents.

As a yoga teacher, I have seen many students struggle with this deceptively challenging position. There is the overworked executive who, after only two minutes, is snoring in the corner. The tense mom, refusing to close her eyes, who stares at the ceiling, ruminating, for the entire 10–20 minutes. The itchy, scratchy, fidgety guy who just can't be still for a second. And I distinctly remember one student telling me after class, "I love yoga. I just hate the deep relaxation at the end. Lying there not doing anything? What a waste of time!" As it turns out, learning to relax, stay awake, and remain fully present is not as easy as it seems.

Although the practice of reclining in the Four Dignities is slightly different from the traditional *Savasana*, there are many similarities. The practice of lying still offers a host of benefits few other activities can boast: profound rejuvenation of body and mind, increased immunity and self-healing capacity, and significant reduction of anxiety and physical pain. In terms of meditation, some spiritual traditions discourage lying down as a meditative practice since the temptation to fall asleep or daydream is much stronger than in other forms of meditation. Individual teachers have gone so far as to say you will not get any benefit from practicing meditation while lying down. It is understandable how certain traditions could come to these conclusions. However, my own experience, and that of many of my students, proves otherwise.

Discovering Reclining Meditation

The first type of meditation I was exposed to was reclining meditation. Throughout my childhood, my mother practiced meditation daily while lying on the couch in our living room.

She never studied meditation formally, but developed her own way of practicing. She would simply tell me, "Honey, I'm going to meditate now." There was no ritual around it, no iconography, no big deal. Then, in the middle of everything, she would lie down and practice for an hour. Sometimes I would watch her. I remember feeling amazed at how she could remain so still, so serene. I used to think that she must go off somewhere really fantastic when she meditated—Heaven maybe. She appeared so peaceful.

One time it looked as if she had stopped breathing. I whispered quietly, "Mom, are you still alive?"

"Yes, dear, I'm just meditating."

She was always immediately present. I remember asking her many times if I was bothering her by running around the house, playing with my friends, or even watching TV in the living room. Her response was always, "No, it's fine. You don't have to worry about disturbing me." As a child, this was perplexing to me.

I understood many years later that it is possible to include all things in one's meditation. Pure awareness, like open space, is all-encompassing. There were no distractions for her because she was not trying to get anywhere or secure any particular mental or spiritual state. Her practice was to remain equally open to whatever arose. Hers was the first method of meditation I learned. Now, more than 30 years later, the things she taught me—mostly by example—continue to form the basis of my personal practice and the foundation of the Four Dignities.

I have met teachers and students in India and the USA who are proud to say they practice seated meditation exclusively. I have listened to them condemn the other three formal positions, expressing fear and doubt about such "lesser practices." The assumption is that by practicing the other positions they will digress, waste their time, or prevent energy from rising up their spine. I've heard people say you're not really meditating if you're walking, lying down, or sitting in a chair. Nonsense.

Meditation can easily become dogmatic—a contrived spiritual act we place over immediate experience. This is a clear sign of striving for something beyond, grasping for something outside our direct experience. According to the View of the Four Dignities, this is a grave mistake. There is an unchecked assumption that we are somehow flawed, incomplete. This assumption must be investigated, dissected. Through self-reflection and insight, we come to realize that everything we seek is already contained in our interrelatedness. As it turns out, we were whole from the beginning. Walking, standing, sitting, or lying down, we are never less than entirely dignified. Our practice is to fully express this dignity unabashedly.

Whatever happens during the practice of reclining is okay. Since we are not striving for anything, and sleep is a perfectly normal expression of our humanness, even if you do fall asleep during your practice, there is no "loss." Actually, this is a fundamental point to understand. There can be no loss so long as we are not seeking any gain. However, if you try to secure a certain mental state, open the chakras, raise the kundalini, or forge some super-human spiritual power, then reclining meditation, and the whole practice of the Four Dignities, will not be a good match for your intent.

With that said, falling asleep during reclining is also not our objective. Our objective is to practice lying still, to fully experience and express this part of our humanness. In short, to relax ambition and be as we are. However, decades of striving to become *this* or *that* can result in deep exhaustion of our energy reserves. When we return home to ourselves and relinquish this type of striving, the storehouse of deep tiredness has a tendency to come up. This is usually when sleepiness takes charge. In my own experience, there were a number of years when it was very difficult to stay awake during seated meditation, not to mention reclining meditation. With time and consistent practice, this phase passed. As our vital energy returns to balance, the practice of reclining spills over with relaxed vitality and innate wakefulness.

Key Skills for Reclining Practice
ALIGNMENT, SURRENDER, WAKEFULNESS.
Alignment

Alignment means learning to organize the joints and limbs of the body through feeling instead of employing learned rules of position. Our objective with alignment is to keep the spine and all the joints in their natural orientation. This sounds easier than it usually is. Chronic tension and years of misalignment can take time and increased awareness to notice and release. As we become more aware, we can feel even the slightest tension or misalignment. The inner work is to correct this, so that naturalness is maintained.

Surrender

Surrender in reclining starts by totally letting Earth hold the weight of the body. Only then can we learn to surrender on the level of mind and breath. Trust is the foundation of surrender. First, we have to let the Earth hold our body. This is trusting solidity. Then we must let clear light awareness hold the mind. This is trusting openness. Finally, we must let the Vital Force breathe through us in its own rhythm. This is trusting primordial creativity. Through trust and surrender, we can let mental doing subside and release control of the breath. Awareness will remain open and non-preferential. Breathing happens by itself. Surrender means emptying completely and letting the divine function.

Wakefulness

Wakefulness is the natural expression of ordinary awareness. Thoughts may come and go like clouds in the sky. Notice how their arrival and departure leave no trace. The sky, without the slightest effort to do so, remains ever open. So it is with the nature of mind. When allowed to be as-it-is, we find that mind is innately open and spontaneously complete. During reclining, we simply allow mind to remain in this natural state of pure enjoyment.

Reclining and the Vertical Axis

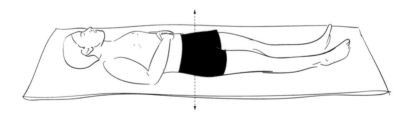

During the practice of lying down, the vertical axis shifts its position in our body by 90 degrees. Instead of running through the length of the body from head to toe, the energy of gravity runs perpendicular to our spine. Energetically speaking, we are much closer to our quadruped friends during reclining. This position gives the organs, muscles, and bones unique access to the Vital Force. Physical and mental rest deeply nourishes us, while gravitational energy performs its own unique function. This is part of the reason why sleeping is so important. Lying down is a kind of plugging in to a particular frequency where Earth and Heaven mix inside our body in the horizontal sphere.

The Reclining Positions

There are two basic groups of reclining meditation positions: lying face up (supine) and lying on your side (fetal). We do not practice lying with the belly toward the floor as this constricts the natural movement of the diaphragm and ribcage, and places strain on the lower back. Among the recommended positions offered below, it is best to experiment with each of the variations until you find the one or two that feel most natural and comfortable to you. Although all of the reclining positions are relaxing and rejuvenating, each of the variations has unique benefits and cautions. Study and experiment with these positions and incorporate your favorites into the compete practice of the Four Dignities.

The Supine Positions

There are two supine positions, each with a slightly different orientation of the hands and upper body. In Position One, the hands rest against the lower belly. In Position Two, the hands rest on the floor, palms facing up. The difference in hand position creates a distinctive alignment of the upper body, which causes subtle changes in breathing. These variations in breathing and alignment evoke distinctive effects and sensations.

Supine Position One: Hands on the Belly

Posture: Position One is practiced lying flat on the back with the palms covering the navel. It is important that the shoulders stay relaxed and the lower back remains neutral. To encourage a neutral alignment of the lumbar spine, slightly tuck the pelvis, reaching the tailbone toward the heels. Then lengthen the legs one at a time, reaching out through the heels. This creates space in the sacrum, hips, and knee joints. Finally, rock the hips from side to side, letting the lower body rest into the most natural and neutral feeling position.

It is health-promoting to lie flat on the floor, or any relatively hard surface, as this encourages proper alignment of the head, torso, and lower limbs. However, if lying completely flat is new for you, there may be a settling-in period as the body returns to its natural alignment. The neck, lower back, and knees are common places discomfort can arise. A thin pillow or folded blanket may be used under the head and neck if there is any discomfort there. A rolled blanket may be placed under the knees if there is any uneasiness in the lower back or knees.

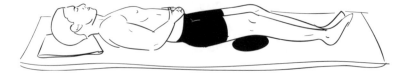

Awareness: Remain with felt-awareness through the body. From head to toe, and from skin to bone, stay with the feeling sensation of the entire body. Stay wakeful in the Center of Being, moment by moment.

Breathing: As with all Four Dignities, we do not exert willful control over the breathing process. We are simply inviting a more natural and unobstructed flow of breath through the whole body. We do this by learning to relax and feel. In Position One, the weight of the hands resting on the belly functions as a source of feedback and gentle massage. With each inhalation, notice the rise of the belly. With each exhalation, notice the fall. Pay attention to the feeling of this movement. Avoid trying to assist the breath by intentionally breathing more deeply.

This practice helps us identify tension anywhere in the abdomen. At the same time, the small pressure created by the weight of the hands sets up a massaging action. The diaphragm presses the abdominal contents toward the pelvis, while the hands exert a downward pressure—not by intentionally pressing, only by their relaxed weight. These two gentle forces work synergistically to help unwind the belly and re-establish Original Breath.

Duration: Sessions can range from five to 60 minutes. For the first 100 days, is it best to practice shorter sessions of 15 minutes or less. Once you are able to fully relax without falling asleep, you can increase the session length.

Unique Benefits: Supine Position One is grounding and centering. It is especially good for developing the diaphragmatic aspect of respiration, drawing breath lower into the lungs and massaging the abdominal organs. The pose improves digestion, assimilation, and elimination, relieves constipation, benefits the reproductive organs, improves memory, addresses chronic fatigue, and helps reduce anxiety and palpitations.

Cautions: Take extra care of the shoulders and lower back. With the hands held against the lower belly, there can be an unconscious tendency to tense the chest and fronts of the shoulders in an effort to keep the hands in place. Make sure to keep the shoulders and chest soft and relaxed. If any discomfort is felt in the lower back, first repeat the lengthening process described in the Posture section above. Then place a rolled blanket or bolster under the knees.

During pregnancy: After the first trimester, prolonged lying in any supine position is contraindicated. Lying flat on the back causes the weight of the baby to press downward, compressing the large blood vessels of the abdomen (abdominal aorta and inferior vena cava). The supine positions may be modified by elevating the upper body with bolsters and blankets to about 45 degrees, or enough that the heart is significantly higher than the belly. The same method of elevating the upper body can also be used by people suffering from acute acid reflux.

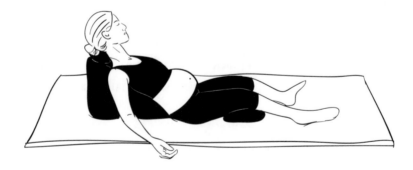

Supine Position Two: Starfish

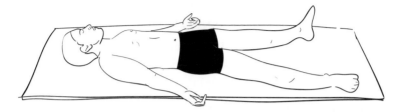

Posture: Starfish is practiced lying flat on the back with the arms at the sides, palms facing upward. This position resembles the traditional Corpse Pose, *Savasana*. As with Position One, we are looking to encourage a neutral alignment of the lumbar spine. To do this, slightly tuck the pelvis, reaching the tailbone toward the heels. Then lengthen the legs one at a time, reaching out through the heels. This creates space in the sacrum, hips, and knee joints. Finally, rock the hips side to side, relaxing all the muscles and letting the lower body rest into the most natural and neutral-feeling position.

Pay attention to the position of the arms. If the arms are too high, the shoulders will tend to tense up. It is best to keep the angle of the arms below the height of the shoulders.

Awareness: After you get settled into the pose, reflect for a moment on the nature of the Unknowable. With the front of the body facing up, there is a profound opportunity to practice surrender to "I don't know." The front of the body is our most vulnerable side. It takes courage to be open here. Embrace the feeling "I don't know." Yield to it, and let a childlike wonder bubble up in you.

Unique Benefits: Starfish is uplifting; it lightens the spirit and develops mindful courage. With the front of the body entirely exposed and open to the sky, Starfish incites a feeling of surrendering to the great unknown. This reawakens basic joy and awe. Physically, the position opens the chest, abdomen, and hips, and reduces congestion and tightness around the lungs, heart, and throat,

Duration: Practice sessions can range from five to 60 minutes. For the first 100 days, it is best to practice shorter sessions of 15 minutes or less. Once you are able to fully relax without falling asleep, you can increase the session length.

Cautions: When it comes to complete relaxation, Starfish is arguably the easier of the two supine positions. However, the tendency to "drift off" or daydream is highest here. Maintain moment-to-moment awareness by continually feeling the changing texture of body and breath. This will induce the deepest states of relaxed Presence, while ensuring the continuity of wakefulness.

During pregnancy: After the first trimester, prolonged lying in any supine position is contraindicated. Lying flat on the back causes the weight of the baby to press downward, compressing the large blood vessels of the abdomen (abdominal aorta and inferior vena cava). Any supine position may be modified by using bolsters or blankets to elevate the upper body to about 45 degrees. The same method of elevating the upper body can also be used by anyone suffering from acute acid reflux (see image on page 156).

The Fetal Positions

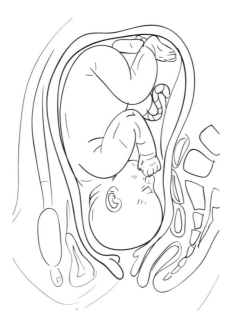

The two fetal positions hint at the posture and alignment of a baby in the womb. With a slightly rounded spine, the front of the body closes in a little bit, creating a profound sense of safety and security indicative of the prenatal state. In Fetal Position One, the left side is toward the floor. In Fetal Position Two, the right side is toward the floor. Each position has a slightly different effect. However, both positions trigger a deep cellular memory of a time when we were suspended in warm fluid and mother took care of everything.

The metaphor behind these two poses is "go back to the womb." This phrase has meaning on micro and macro levels. Inwardly, our practice is to return to the Center of Being deep in our belly. In this case, "womb" represents the place we hold our innermost essence. In certain Daoist traditions, practitioners visualize carrying a miniature version of themselves in their belly (*dantien*). It's a spiritual pregnancy. The idea here is that our prenatal essence or Original Nature is found more in the belly (feeling) than in the head (thinking). Although we are not visualizing anything per se, the practice of moving our sense of Presence from the head to the belly is a kind of "returning to the womb" on the micro level.

On the macro level, we can observe how each living thing arises within a field of life energy (prana or qi). Like fish in the ocean, we are submerged in the matrix of living energy. It permeates and animates every aspect of our being. "Going back to the womb," in this case, means becoming conscious of the nurturing quality of the universal life force. Wherever we happen to be, we are always in the center of nature's belly.

Fetal Position One: The Solar Position

Posture: Lie on your left side in a fetal position. Maintain length in the spine while allowing the back to round a little. Place a small pillow or folded blanket under your head, with the left hand cupping the left ear. The right hand rests on the belly or upper hip/thigh. The left knee bends a little more than the right. This allows the inside of the right knee to rest in the fleshy pocket at the inner top portion of the left calf muscle. This leg alignment prevents the discomfort that can occur if the bony parts of the inner knee joints rest against one another.

Awareness: Enter the womb of direct experience. Feel your body from skin to bone bathed in universal life energy. Feel the natural rhythm of your breathing. Remain awake and at ease. Know that all is indeed exactly as it needs to be.

Breathing: Because the left side of the body is lower than the right in this position, gravity causes more blood to move down into the left side of the body. After a few minutes, the left nostril begins to constrict slightly and the right nostril starts to open. The breathing automatically shifts primarily to the right nostril. As with all the positions, we simply relax and allow the process of breathing to happen by itself.

Duration: Sessions can range from five to 30 minutes. Many people find that it's easier to fall asleep in the fetal position. For the first 100 days, or until you can remain relaxed and alert in the position, it is best to practice shorter sessions of 15 minutes or less. Once you are able to fully relax without falling asleep, you can increase the session length.

Unique Benefits: The Solar Position is warming and nourishing; it regulates metabolic heat (digestive fire) and is especially beneficial for people with cold-related conditions or a cold-deficient type of constitution.

Cautions: People with excessive heat conditions[17] or an over-stimulated nervous system might benefit more from practicing the Lunar Position. If you are pregnant, ask your doctor or midwife which side they recommend lying on. It may be a matter of professional or personal opinion, but it is good to note that there are varying ideas about which side is best to lie on during pregnancy. When in doubt, trust your inner guidance.

Fetal Position Two: The Lunar Position

Posture: Lie on your right side in a fetal position. Maintain length in the spine while allowing the back to round a little. Place a small pillow or folded blanket under your head, with the right hand cupping the right ear. The left hand rests on the belly or upper hip/thigh. The right knee bends a little more than the left. This allows the inside of the left knee to rest in the fleshy pocket at the inner top portion of the right calf muscle. This leg alignment prevents the discomfort that can occur if the bony parts of the inner knee joints rest against one another.

Breathing: Because the right side of the body is lower than the left in this position, gravity causes more blood to move down into the right side of the body. After a few minutes, the right nostril begins to constrict slightly and the left nostril starts to open. The breathing automatically shifts primarily to the left nostril. Our objective with breathing is to allow the Original Breath to function freely. The pose itself will regulate breathing. Our job is to relax and let it happen.

Duration: Sessions can range from five to 30 minutes. Many people find that it's easier to fall asleep in the fetal positions. For the first 100 days, or until you can remain relaxed and alert in this position, is it best to practice shorter sessions of 15 minutes or less. Once you are able to fully relax without falling asleep, you can increase the session length.

Unique Benefits: The Lunar Position is cooling and calming; it regulates distribution of fluids (blood, lymph, sweat, etc.) and is especially beneficial for people with heat conditions, or a hot-excessive type constitution.

Cautions: People with deficient cold conditions[18] might benefit more from practicing the Solar Position instead. If you are pregnant, please ask your doctor or midwife which side they recommend lying on. It might be a matter of professional or personal opinion; however, it is prudent to note that there are varying ideas about which side is best to lie on during the three trimesters of pregnancy. When in doubt, trust your inner guidance.

꙾ Chapter 9 ꙾

THE COMPLETE
PRACTICE

"Walking, standing, sitting or lying—all behavior
and activity are plainness, even to the extent that
when one encounters any sorrowful or joyful event,
the mind remains unwavering."

Bodhidharma Anthologies

Now that we understand each of the Four Dignities individually,
it is time to bring the four into one complete practice. In this
section, we delve into the practical considerations involved
in implementing your own daily practice: where to practice,
what to wear, the best times for practice, and tools to support
you. However, the most essential aspect of a complete practice
is connecting View, Method, and Fruition. Of these three,
understanding the View is the most crucial. It is not only what

you do in your cultivation, but also how you internalize and express your practice within circumstances of your life.

Four as One

Performed as a set, the Four Dignities create a complete practice that proves greater than the sum of its parts. The four individual positions may be sequenced in a number of ways. The most commonly used progression is:

Walking > Standing > Sitting > Reclining

This series may be done at any time of the day with good results. We call it the Root Sequence. The progression moves from the most physically active position to the least. Even though all four are quite gentle, we understand their effects relative to one another. Energetically, we can describe this as moving from *yang* to *yin*.

Starting a session with walking is a great way to limber the joints and warm the body. Because walking demands a higher degree of physical coordination than the other Dignities, it also brings the mind into a state of relaxed alertness. For most people, standing is the most physically challenging of the four. Walking before standing is good to relax and enliven the muscles. Sitting after standing builds Presence, while affording a deserved break from the physical demands of standing. Finishing with lying down brings the whole sequence into its most tranquil state.

In the Root Sequence, lying down serves as the culmination of the practice. It is here that the whole set comes together. Lying down is clearly the least physically challenging of the four. Yet, for most students, it poses the greatest challenge in maintaining alertness and embodied Presence. At the end of the sequence, the mind has had a chance to settle and the body is ready for deeper relaxation.

Becoming accustomed to maintaining stillness while standing, sitting, and lying down can be challenging for some people in the beginning. If the Root Sequence proves too challenging at first, you might try an alternate sequence with extra walking. The following progression introduces movement between each of the still postures. It looks like this:

Walking > Standing > Walking > Sitting > Walking > Reclining

If you elect to do this variation, make each of the walking sections roughly one-third of the time of the other three Dignities. For example: Walk for two minutes, stand for six minutes, walk for two minutes, sit for six minutes, walk for two minutes, lie down for six minutes. This would be a 24-minute practice. If you find the stillness aspect of meditation more challenging, you may notice this helps you settle into the practice with less effort. There is a trade-off, however. The simple elegance of the Root Sequence is sacrificed here in favor of more movement. Simplicity gives way to the benefit of increased movement. It's a give and take.

The transitions between Dignities are best kept natural and organic. The key is to be mindful and deliberate, yet not mechanical or overly formal. If any transition or position feels forced, explore subtle adjustments in your posture until you find a more instinctive way of doing it. With time and repetition, your practice will become a seamless dance. The transitions and Dignities themselves merge into one complete expression. This kind of proficiency cannot be rushed or manufactured. It results naturally from sincere cultivation.

"When you do something, you should burn yourself up completely, like a good bonfire, leaving no trace of yourself."
Suzuki Roshi

What to Wear

Comfort is essential. It is ideal to wear loose-fitting clothing made of natural fabrics. This will allow the body to breathe and move without restriction. It also helps maintain a comfortable body temperature. Clothing that constricts the body in any one place will affect the flow of blood through the whole system. This subtle detail can make a big difference in your practice.

Maintain an even temperature. Some people find they feel cooler during practice due to the relative state of relaxation. Other people feel quite warm as the Vital Force begins to flow more evenly. The important point is to dress appropriately for your constitution and environment to avoid getting too cold or too hot.

When to Practice

For formal meditation practice, early morning and late evening are the times traditionally recommended. The early morning, between the hours of 4 and 8 a.m., is a particularly beneficial time. The environmental energy is gentle and fresh during these hours. The rising Sun is not too strong and the world is still moving relatively slowly. A morning session is a great way to vitalize body and mind, and start the day centered and present. The evening time, after our worldly affairs are complete, is another nice time to practice. At this time, the Sun has set and we can more readily turn attention to our cultivation. An evening session of practice will also serve to improve quality of sleep.

Although practicing during these two traditional times is considered ideal, we each must find the time that best suits our lifestyle. To encourage consistent and sincere practice, it's best to find the time that is most realistic within your daily routine. This also means making your practice a priority. If we hope to *find* time to practice, it will scarcely happen. If are to have the time for cultivation, we have to *make* it. When we honestly commit to daily practice, we find that the whole universe seems to accommodate and support our cultivation.

Since the Four Dignities work with the body's energy systems, practicing right after eating can cause discomfort and even indigestion. It is best to wait at least an hour after a meal to start practicing; two to three hours would be better. Food may be taken in as little as ten minutes after practice, although 30 minutes would be ideal. It is also important to avoid cold drinks before or after practice. A little hot or warm water is best. In the hot season, room temperature water is fine.

Where to Practice

It is helpful to have a quiet, clean, and private space. An uncluttered room indoors is usually ideal. Walking may be practiced outdoors, but for sitting, standing, and lying down it is recommended to practice inside. If you can practice in the same indoor place every day, this is helpful, especially in the first few years. If your life situation does not afford such a luxury, don't worry about it. Consistency reigns supreme over convenience. After your practice is stable, location will not matter much. You can practice just about anywhere. Most importantly, do not practice in a windy place, or even where there is a draft from an open window. Windows may be opened before and after practice to freshen the air. During practice, it is best to keep windows closed.

Tools for Practice

You do not need any special equipment to practice the Four Dignities. However, there are a few simple things that make the practice more comfortable and convenient: a meditation cushion, a yoga blanket or two, a shawl, and a good pair of "barefoot shoes."

For outdoor walking in warmer months, going barefoot is wonderful. In the cold season, wearing anatomically designed flat-soled shoes is best. Shoes with lifted heels or narrow toe boxes alter our Original Posture and change our natural gait. Most conventional shoes are restrictive and overbuilt. There are many choices for shoes made to replicate the experience of barefoot walking. Although no shoe can truly replicate actually walking barefoot, technology has come a long way in understanding how to engineer a shoe that lets the feet function naturally.

If you are new to this blossoming area of research, you can learn more by searching for "barefoot shoes" or "minimalist shoes." There is a wealth of great information online as to the benefits of going barefoot and/or switching to "barefoot shoes."

For standing practice, if the floor is wood or tile, it can get pretty cold in the winter. Socks might not be enough to protect the cold from entering your feet. In this case, you can wear some thin-soled slippers. Make sure they're flat. The ones traditionally used for Taiji practice work well.

For sitting practice, as we have mentioned, it is critical that the hips be higher than the knees. This allows the spine to remain in its natural position. To maintain Original Posture while sitting, a meditation cushion or kneeling bench is ideal. If sitting on the floor is not comfortable or possible, a chair will work just as well. A chair made of natural material would be preferred. And one that you dedicate solely to meditation practice would be best. A yoga blanket may be used on the seat of the chair to pad the sitting bones and elevate the hips to the proper height. A shawl is nice to have to wrap lightly around the body during sitting. This provides a sense of safety and support, and keeps the body warm in cooler months.

For lying down, the yoga blanket/s may be used in a few different ways. It is nice to cover up with a blanket if the room feels cool. If the lower back feels tender, you can roll the blanket and place it under the knees. In the warmer months, a light shawl may be used to cover up with. This keeps the body warm and provides a sense of security that lets the subconscious mind be more at ease.

Again, these props are nice to have, but they are not indispensable. Never let the lack of props deter you from continuing your practice.

Timescale for Practice

Below is a sample timescale for designing a formal practice of the Four Dignities as a complete set. A five-minute practice of each Four is considered foundational. Twenty minutes of total practice is the minimum amount of time it takes most people to fully "drop in." A nine-minute practice of each Four is considered transitional, meaning the practice is beginning to develop some solidity. A 15-minute practice of each Four is considered a solid practice. Beyond 15 minutes, time may be added as desired. However, consistency is more important than adding time to your practice. A shorter practice realistically performed each day is superior to longer sessions done sporadically. Develop your practice based on your level of interest, commitment, and lifestyle.

SAMPLE SEQUENCES

Root Sequence:

Walking > Standing > Sitting > Reclining > Closing

Root Sequence with Extra Walking:

Walking > Standing > Walking > Sitting > Walking > Reclining > Closing

---

SAMPLE PRACTICE TIMES

5 minutes x 4 Dignities = 20 minutes

6 minutes x 4 = 24 minutes

7 minutes x 4 = 28 minutes

8 minutes x 4 = 32 minutes

9 minutes x 4 = 36 minutes

10 minutes x 4 = 40 minutes

15 minutes x 4 = 60 minutes

20 minutes x 4 = 80 minutes

The Closing Sequence

At the end of each practice session, a short closing sequence is performed. The closing serves to seal in the effects of the practice and dedicate the benefit to all beings. This important process is sometimes called "harvesting and distributing." Harvesting the fruit of the practice is a process of five simple steps: rubbing the skin, clicking the teeth, circling the tongue inside the mouth, swishing saliva, and swallowing saliva.

Distributing the benefit is the last thing we do at the end of the closing. This step is employed to reduce the tendency of "I" to mistakenly think the benefit of spiritual practice is for "me." Offering the benefit is a time-tested way of cultivating compassion and keeping ego-clinging in check.

During the practice of the Four Dignities, or any yogic discipline, our energetic field expands and becomes more dispersed. This happens naturally as we settle into embodied Presence and return to Original Breath. This expanded energetic state is deeply healing for body and mind. However, at the conclusion of practice it is important to consolidate that expansion back to the physical body. This strengthens our internal organs and bones, and prevents the feeling of spaciness that can result from incorrect application of yogic techniques.

In Chinese systems of self-cultivation (*qigong, daoyin,* or *yang sheng*), rubbing the skin is called "qi washing" or "dry washing." It is used morning and evening as a method of self-care and as an overall health tonic. This powerful practice normalizes and bolsters the body's vital energy by stimulating the largest organ of the body, the skin. Energetically, we can understand this effect as harmonizing the *wei qi* (Chinese "external energy") or *vyana vayu* (Sanskrit "all-pervading energy"). Dry washing is highly praised in the oral traditions of India, China, and Tibet, and mentioned in traditional yoga texts such as the *Shiva Samhita* and *Hatha Yoga Pradipika*. The exercise of thorough rubbing of the skin is a common practice among the many yogic traditions throughout Asia. The hands are an extension of the heart, and attentively rubbing each part of the body is powerful medicine. This is important to do after each session of practice, or anytime one perspires from yogic exercise. The Four Dignities practice is physically gentle, yet it produces a certain amount of internal heat. This heat may or may not cause you to lightly perspire. Whether or not you perspire, remember to always rub the skin at the end of each practice.

"The perspiration arising from practice
should be rubbed into the body (and not wiped),
as by so doing the body becomes strong."

Hatha Yoga Pradipika

Harvesting the Fruit
Rub

Rub the hands together until they are warm. This activates the session of qi washing. Then continue rubbing every part of the body with equal pressure. You don't have to press hard, just enough to stimulate the skin. The key is to be thorough. Don't forget the hidden places, such as between the toes and fingers, behind the ears, the sacrum, and groin. Also, make sure to rub as much of your back as you can reach. Challenge yourself to touch every part of your back. This limbers the shoulders and opens the ribcage. You can practice rubbing over your clothes or directly on bare skin. If the weather and location permit, qi washing directly on bare skin is always best. Finish by rubbing the belly in a circular motion while smiling.

Click

Click the teeth together gently 36 times. This stimulates and strengthens the roots of the teeth, jaw, brain, and bones. Make sure to feel the vibration through all the teeth, top and bottom, front and back.

Lick

Lick the teeth repeatedly until copious saliva flows. Keep the mouth closed, and lick the top and bottom teeth, front and back. This stimulates the parasympathetic nervous response (the rest and renew reflex), improves digestion, and strengthens the body's self-healing power.

Swish

Swish the saliva in the mouth vigorously 36 times without swallowing. Swishing your saliva stimulates the release of beneficial enzymes and hormones, and helps to balance the thyroid gland.

Swallow

Swallow the saliva in three strong gulps. As if you were swallowing three pearls of light, feel the sensation of the saliva going straight from your mouth to the lower belly. This consolidates and stores the Vital Force in the Center of Being. Rest in stillness for a moment. Notice the feeling in your belly and throughout your body.

Harvesting the Fruit Mantra

Rub. Click. Lick. Swish. Swallow.

Dedicate the Benefit

This is the conclusion of our practice. It is important to make the dedication heartfelt and sincere. Begin by joining the palms together in front of the chest. Expand your awareness to include all living things: plants, animals, human beings, Sun, Moon, stars, planets, water, fire, wind, and all the forces of nature. Arouse the sincere wish to see all beings happy and free. Remember, "all beings" includes you, too. Radiate kindness and goodwill in all directions.

Then, as you separate your hands, imagine releasing a bird into the open space. In your mind's eye, see this bird soaring high and free. This is a symbol that peace has been established in the ten directions.

The session of practice is now complete.

THE FOUR STEPS OF PRACTICE

1. Contemplate the View.
2. Walk. Stand. Sit. Lie Down.
3. Rub. Click. Lick. Swish. Swallow.
4. Dedicate the Benefit.

Practice Poem

Many spiritual traditions use pithy instructions to remind practitioners of the essential points of View and Method. These instructions are commonly rendered in poetic verse, mantra, or song. The poem below is a piece I wrote for my students. It may be read at the beginning of each practice session.

Twenty-Four Lines to Clarify the View

Start precisely where you are, nowhere else.
Unsheathe the sword of self-honesty;
Cut away laziness, ambition, and contrivance.
Do not squander this precious human life;
Conditions will never be more favorable.

Wake up!
Do not delude yourself by thinking, "I will practice tomorrow."
It never happens!
Gather your resolve; take up the Vajra Seat right now.

Establish the base; firm like a mountain.
Elongate the spine; filling the space between Heaven and Earth.
Eyes horizontal, nose vertical; face serene, like an alpine pond.

Do not tamper with Original Breath; let life breathe itself.
Do not tamper with Original Nature; be as you are.

Practice for no other reason than to practice.

Renounce your addiction to pleasure and convenience.
Drop preferences and give up cleverness.
Relinquish all interest in personal gain.
With unflinching courage, directly enter Openness.

From skin to bone...feel.

Simply leave body and mind untamed;
Take refuge in luminous space.
Remain centered deep in the belly,
And then forget that you are there.

Part III

FRUITION

"Be aware that the Buddhas and Ancestors repeatedly taught that we must not be slack in our training and practice, so that we do not stain or tarnish our innate enlightenment, which is inseparable from our practice."

Dogen

Fruition arises through the interaction of View and Method. The word "fruition" originates from the Latin *fructus* ("fruit") and *frui* ("to enjoy"). When our View (way of seeing) and Method (way of going about things) are in harmony with natural law, we harvest the fruit of spontaneous enjoyment.

Our human situation is not so different from that of a mango tree. A mango tree gives mangoes without intending to do so. It does not decide between giving cherries, apples, or mangoes. According to its nature, the tree relates to its immediate environment. It engages with soil, air, Sun, rain. Through the process of simply being what it is, the mango tree bears its fruit. A ripening mango on the branch probably has no idea how delicious it is. And the tree has no framework for understanding what an accomplishment it has achieved.

To think of Fruition as "personal benefit" is misleading. Such a notion results from the cosmology of insufficiency. Fruition is being what we naturally are, nothing more and nothing less. It is the simplest and most elusive thing.

Chapter 10

THE FRUITS OF OUR ACTIONS

"Life is fragile, like a dewdrop poised on the tip of a blade of grass, ready to be carried away by the first breath of morning breeze. It is not enough just to have a sincere desire to practice the Dharma and the intention to begin soon. Do not just passively wait for the wind of death to carry away your plans before you have gotten around to them. As soon as the idea of practicing comes to you, do it without hesitation."

Dilgo Khyentse Rinpoche

Becoming a Practitioner

The basic point of the Four Dignities is to express Original Nature and harmonize with the immediate situation. It is important to remember that we are not chasing away thoughts or suppressing any experience. We are not attempting to secure states of consciousness according to our preference. We are remaining quite natural. Spontaneously, everything goes its own way. This is why we place importance on feeling body and breath. The feeling texture of the experience of body and breath is constantly changing and self-resolving. By knowing this through our own experience, we begin to understand the suchness of all things.

To this end, it is crucial that we distinguish between struggle and discipline. The former is unnecessary, the latter indispensable. To practice now and again, when we feel moved to do so, is quite easy. However, to become a practitioner is something altogether different. A practitioner is someone who understands the essence and value of discipline. Unfortunately, in our culture of entitlement, the word "discipline" has fallen out of fashion. It is often interpreted as dutifully doing things one would rather not have to do. It carries a hint of obligation, punishment even.

I had one student who related to the idea of discipline as having to follow the commands of her "inner Catholic school teacher." She would rebel against her own practice in an effort to "show that old hag who is boss." The idea of keeping a discipline felt like torment to her. This continued until she investigated her assumptions and discovered the cause of her inner conflict.

In religious, political, and academic contexts, discipline is laden with "should" and "ought," and often makes people feel wrong about the way they naturally are. The culturally promoted version of discipline usually coincides with guilt and shame. Under social pressure, one can easily resign oneself to "jumping through hoops" in pursuit of success, societal acceptance, and so on. In the process, one develops a disdain for discipline. Understandably. The need to act contrary to our nature is demeaning. Yet the fault does not lie with discipline, but in its misuse.

To avoid the feeling of being manipulated or restrained, many spiritual practitioners wrestle with discipline for decades. It is easy to get caught in the reactive phase that follows breaking free from the controlling forces of parents, teachers, or religious leaders. Freedom is commonly misunderstood as doing whatever one pleases. This is a juvenile use of freedom. To mature on the Path, we must come full circle and rediscover discipline in a new light.

To have any kind of Fruition in our practice, we have to reinstate discipline to its rightful place. Free of dogma and obligation, discipline is an empowered choice. It is a quantum leap beyond the dualism of whimsical liberty versus mindless adherence. Discipline is a commitment to get to the heart of the matter of self-cultivation. It is where the rubber meets the road. The Way is illusive and slippery. Discipline is our primary means of maintaining traction.

It comes down to practice. The three most important times to practice are when we want to, when we don't want to, and when we feel ambivalent. In other words, a practitioner understands the law of continuity. They see it confirmed all around them: how seasons turn, how day follows night, how the cosmic song never skips a beat. The definition of true practice is constancy. The Sun never misses a day of shining. A practitioner takes their cue from the Sun and expresses their practice at least once in every 24-hour period.

To move along with the way things move along, that is our Way. Over weeks, months, and years, we come to understand that the simple act of continuity is Original Nature itself. Freedom is not totally free. Each thing is bound to its nature. Because luminous space is continuously open, and Vital Force cannot be created or destroyed, true practice has no beginning or end.

To become true practitioners, we must relinquish all interest in personal gain, including any secret fantasies of bliss, freedom, salvation, transcendence, or enlightenment. As the Zen saying goes, "Only don't know." This means admitting complete defeat, total surrender. Since we don't know what we are, where we are going, or what's happening here, how could we claim to know how to untangle the knot of ego-clinging, much less how to upgrade nature's design?

The intent to improve is a slippery slope. Clever concepts are ego's hook; however appealing, they always snag us. We must wake up and learn to see the barbed catch hidden inside the bait. We must not fall for the promise of gaining benefit from spiritual practice. This type of grasping comes from inner poverty. Practice only because you must, because that is what practitioners do. Practice simply to practice. Sit only to sit. Walk only to walk. Empty yourself completely and let the divine function.

One-Act Samadhi

Each action is complete unto itself. Walking. Standing. Sitting. Lying down. Each act is so complete that not a single thing is lacking. In a moment of just standing, there is only standing. Nothing can be done now to produce lasting satisfaction later. Conditions are always shifting; the future is uncertain. If basic joy is not realized within the framework of this-here-now, it will not be found anywhere. This is not to imply that cause and effect are not operative, only that Fruition cannot be found within such a duality. Fruition is found in the midst of embodied Presence. It is not the *result* of Presence that is fruitful, but Presence itself *is* the fruit. Our practice is to express suchness with each act. This is true wealth. To carry out every gesture from the seat of intrinsic wholeness is to have everything already within your Being. This is majesty. This is inner richness. This is how we can express Original Nature in every circumstance.

Fruition is simple, yet elusive. If we try to "get it," it is gone. If we do not attend to our practice diligently, Fruition is nowhere to be found. Doing and not doing are both mistakes. Doing assumes a doer; we are caught in egoism. Not doing is a withdrawal from life; we are caught in entropy, falling to the lowest common denominator. If we act from wanting, we express inner poverty. If we pull back from engaging the immediate situation, we experience a separation from Being. Such is the spiritual pickle.

In non-doing, there is only the act. One stroke of the brush. One strike of the sword. One chance meeting with an old friend. A true practitioner gives equal importance to each action. Washing the dishes is equal in status to embracing one's lover. There are no mundane moments. This is part of the reason why we take four ordinary activities and utilize them as formal practice. The spirit of this simplicity and honesty spills over into every other aspect of life.

A sincere follower of the Way must eventually set aside all spiritual toys and settle into unembellished immediate Presence. There is no particular thing, teacher, or circumstance that can produce this. It is available only when our full attention relaxes into savoring complete experience. Daoists call this "free and easy wandering." It is an attitude of straightforwardness. We eschew grand ideals and meet life from a place of genuine humanness.

The Paradox of Doubt

As our practice unfolds, clarity naturally dawns, and we see the hidden lies in so many things. Religion. There is so much to be doubtful about. History. Politics. Academia. Science. Medicine. Personal agenda too often distorts the truth. Much of what we've been taught is simply not so. With clarity, a great doubt arises. We learn to distrust the authority of even our own thoughts. The basis of thinking is rooted in givens, concepts pre-established by our culture's worldview. Freedom from identification with your own thoughts is a healthy sign that the knot of self-delusion is untangling.

However, doubt is incomplete without its partner. At some point we must come full circle and rediscover doubtlessness. After the initial stage of awakening matures, the usefulness of doubt wanes. To rely on doubt exclusively produces a new kind of cleverness. Spiritual cynicism. "I'm too awake to be tricked by dogma and spiritual fantasy. I don't believe in anything anymore." Although this kind of razor sharpness is helpful in not falling prey to spiritual materialism, it becomes a new kind of guarding, a new limitation. It causes the heart to close. Doubt gone stale turns out to be the greatest undermining force for mature spiritual practitioners. Becoming doubtless is the next step we must take. This requires even more audacity.

There is only one way to become doubtless. Contrary to popular assumption, belief is not the way. Anything that requires faith is somehow defective. The need to believe co-arises with the intuitive sense that belief is contrived. We are always aware that we do not know. Rather than admit, "I don't know," we try to silence this non-knowing with the boisterous voice of conviction. Belief requires a corresponding concept. Concepts are mind-made models of an incomprehensible reality. They are incomplete and will never fully represent the totality of reality as-it-is.

Behind extreme confidence is extreme doubt. Outward display of conviction always co-arises with secret inward doubt. Self-doubt. Perhaps this is most obvious in fundamentalism. With a quick scan of history, it is easy to see how belief in ideas, especially ones set forth by charismatic leaders, can disengage people from their humanity. Under the spell of concepts, people easily lose their human-heartedness. Ideals are a block to feeling. Feeling is our umbilical cord to basic sanity.

An honest seeker must go directly to the one thing they can actually be certain about. Certainty must come from our own direct experience, nowhere else. No book, teacher, or doctrine has any business here. This is an intimate and personal meeting between you and the great Unknowable. All spiritual paths lead here: to the moment you confront what mystics call Divine Ignorance. You must, once and for all, know that you do not know. You must realize that the observer, limited to the point of view of "I," cannot comprehend the whole of reality. Only when the certainty of "I don't know" dawns will you become truly doubtless.

It is disastrously ironic that the one thing that can restore true courage and establish doubtlessness is "I don't know." This is the antithesis of what religion, politics, academia, and advertising have so desperately propagated. Our cultural addiction to ego-glorification makes the story seem believable. Self-cherishing lives within the domain of the hope-faith-doubt-belief conflict. This is the proverbial struggle of good and evil, based in the erroneous assumption of a divided world. God above. Hell below. Carnal desire. Spiritual aspiration. Such distinctions only exist in the mind.

To place full confidence in "I don't know," and to no longer harbor the secret feeling that something is wrong with you because of it, is the great leap beyond illusion. It opens the gateway to doubtlessness. Once you are doubtless about the fact that you do not know, you can discard hope, faith, belief, and all other spiritual playthings that once kept you distracted from the suchness of your situation.

With doubtlessness you are free to play the ball where it lands. Self-honesty is your guiding force. Unfettered by the exhausting game of needing to conceal your doubt with cleverness and contrived confidence, you can actually live your life with unprecedented openness. You come to understand that conflict is resolved within the all-encompassing space of the unguarded human heart.

> "Keep a close eye on what you are accumulating in order to know the tendencies toward fortune or misfortune."
>
> *Huainanzi*

Obstacles on the Path

The things we imagine to be obstructing our awakening are also part of the mirage. Strictly speaking, there are no true obstacles on the Path. There is only accumulation through repetition. Whatever we repeat becomes stronger.

Original Posture is like a mountain. No matter what transpires on or around the mountain, it remains a mountain. Original Breath is like the turning of the seasons. The natural rhythm is unstoppable. Original Nature is like the sky. There is not a single thing that could obstruct its openness. Clouds come and go. Thunder, lightning, and rain come and go. The sky remains absolutely pristine and untarnished, no matter what moves through it. The nature of body, breath, and mind are just like this.

Even though no obstacle whatsoever exists, we might encounter the experience of feeling blocked or stuck from time to time. Understand that such an experience is based on perception. It has no intrinsic reality itself. Circumstances are circumstances. It is judging mind that divides situations into "favorable" and "unfavorable." It is the habit of giving fixed name and form to that which is fundamentally empty that produces the appearance of obstacles. The old snake in the rope mistake again!

The habit of forcing our projections on experience is a type of aggression. Water takes the shape of its container without hesitation. Open space accepts whatever is placed inside it. Obstacles exist in the realm of mind only. Mind, with its preconceived agenda, perceives the world as a difficulty to be overcome on the way to getting what it wants. This is not to say that challenges will not present themselves. For a practitioner, however, challenges are opportunities to express creativity and spontaneity. They are not excuses to unleash aggression.

On its journey from the high Himalayas to the Bay of Bengal, the river Ganges meets many challenges. No matter what the situation presents, the Ganges finds a way to keep flowing toward the sea. The river never pulls back from the circumstances it encounters. It never retreats into itself. Nor does it use brute force to succeed. It is through intimacy and gentle persistence that the river stays its path.

Gentleness is one of the most important aspects of Four Dignities training. An honest practitioner, time and time again, rejects aggression when challenges arise. Gentleness is not to be confused with weakness. Soft water carves a deep canyon into solid granite. Gentleness is the most powerful weapon of a spiritual warrior. Through intimacy, understanding, and gentleness, the spiritual adept conquers all would-be obstacles.

The Conundrum of Freedom

It is possible to be without the limiting constraints of self-consciousness, anxiety, and claustrophobia. It is possible to be free of the feeling of separation that results from identification with a finite personal reference point. Yet this freedom is not a license for reckless abandon. Freedom is not the liberty to do whatever one pleases. This type of freedom usually coincides with profound suffering; it is motivated by egoism. As much as our over-indulgent culture would have us believe otherwise, immediate and unrestrained gratification of personal desire does not bring lasting joy to the heart. In fact, in the long run, it serves to increase suffering.

So, what is true freedom?

As human beings, the open dimension of our experience allows for a vast range of conduct. This range is significantly more diverse than that of any other living organism we know of. Yet the ability to do anything we want might be more of a liability than an asset when it comes to satisfaction. Ignorant of the repercussions of our choices, we exercise one of the most precarious powers we have: free will. Seemingly limitless are the possibilities of what we can do. We often do things "just because we can." We can eat too much, drink too much, work too much, and stay up too late. We can clone sheep and grow hamburgers from stem cells. We can make nuclear weapons that can destroy the entire planet. Ego believes itself to be a god.

God or not, each action has its repercussions. The law of cause and effect is operative. Ignorance says, "I'll do everything I can because I want to see what I am capable of. I don't care about the consequences." Wisdom says, "I will do only what nourishes life and minimizes suffering." This is the highest use of free will.

Freedom is a great power that can easily be squandered. Through our practice, we come to realize that we cannot be lax in our relationship to freedom. Direct realization of inner freedom coincides with a firm adherence to upright conduct, routine, and respect for natural law. Quite different from morally imposed religious rules, these are natural expressions of wholesomeness. Centered in basic goodness, our actions accord naturally with what supports life. No outwardly imposed rules or idealized moral conduct are needed. When ignorance and deceit are given up, people return to a good and simple life.

By dwelling in the Center of Being, we know instinctively what virtue is. Behavior that may look like strict discipline from the outside often occurs as spontaneous action for a highly cultivated person. When there is ample space within, one feels great joy in flowing along with the natural course of things. What, in the beginning, we might call discipline turns out to be more like rhythm. Dynamic. Changing. Summer follows spring. Night follows day. Exhale follows inhale. An adept moves like a river, changes with the landscape. This is freedom.

The Healing Power of Vital Force

When I was about eight years old, I got a new bicycle for my birthday. One afternoon, I went into the garage to clean the bicycle and oil the chain. I turned the bike upside down, resting it on the seat and handlebars, and began to oil the chain. I turned the sprocket round and round to oil each link. After I finished, I wanted to see how fast I could get the back wheel going. As I turned the cranks faster and faster, the bike became unstable. When it finally tipped, I reached to catch the bike, and my left index finger got caught between the chain and the teeth of the turning sprocket.

Moments later, I was on the way to the emergency room. The tip of my finger had been badly severed. The doctor numbed my hand, cleaned the wound, and stitched everything back together. He told me it would leave a nasty scar, and that I might lose feeling in the tip of that finger. He sent me home with a sizable bandage and a prescription for painkillers. His work was done.

Over the next few weeks, the flesh grew back together and the outer wound healed. There was still pain and numbness. Over the next six months, the nerves became less painful but the numbness persisted. Over the next decade, the scar almost completely disappeared and the pain and numbness went away.

How did the body know exactly how to restore the skin tissue, nerves, blood vessels, and fingernail? How does the body grow itself back to the original form? The doctor didn't make that happen. I didn't either. No external medicine caused the body to heal itself. There is an intrinsic intelligence within the body, within nature, that is always operative. It nurtures life and attempts to return all things to original wholeness.

The injured finger is but a minor incident. Countless are the stories of miraculous healing. Innumerable are the documented cases of full recovery from "fatal disease" and the regrowth of tissue that, supposedly, once damaged, cannot be repaired. This is the power of Vital Force. There exists an energetic blueprint for each living thing. The Vital Force constantly flows through these blueprints to maintain the unique function of each life form.

The miracle of self-healing is an inborn trait of Nature. There is nothing we need to do to improve it, and nothing we can do to make it happen. It is a matter of getting out of the way. This is one reason why our cultivation of Original Posture, Original Breath, and Original Nature is so valuable. Through the practice of the Four Dignities, we learn to identify and release conditioned ways of moving, breathing, and being. We work to remove interference. Conditioning that is not inherently contained in our blueprint distorts the flow of Vital Force. As we drop accumulated mental, emotional, and physical tension, the life energy flourishes within, nourishing every fiber of our being. This allows the miracle of self-healing to happen unhampered.

> "Maintaining order rather than correcting disorder is the ultimate principle of wisdom. To cure disease after it has appeared is like digging a well when one already feels thirsty, or forging weapons after the war has already begun."
>
> *Nei Jing*[19]

In terms of chronic illness or lingering health conditions, the foundation of self-healing is the realization that illness does not come from outside of us. Chronic ailments are a call to pay closer attention. Simply put, healing is loving what has not been loved yet.

Every aspect of our life is calling for our genuine attendance. Our Presence is requested. Presence is what our kids want, what our lovers want, what our elders want. Any part of our life that lacks this honest attention will start to act up. This rule applies to all aspects of our life: physical, mental, emotional, spiritual, sexual, financial, domestic. Facing ourselves means embracing our complete situation, showing up wholeheartedly.

Entering the Forest

Certainty and comfort must be left at the edge of the forest. Innumerable changing circumstances afford endless opportunities for applying our awakening. There is no such thing as mastery. Wisdom cannot be found in information. We have to apply what we know in our own daily life to embody what is true and virtuous. This is engaged spirituality. The conditions have never been more ideal for awakened action. Gather your courage and resolve, discard bargaining and excuses, and just do it!

As our formal practice matures, it will naturally spill over into all aspects of our life. We find ourselves practicing the Four Dignities in everything we do. Sitting on the subway becomes a practice. Standing in line at the grocery store becomes a practice. In a sense, our practice has gone beyond the confines of a specific time and space. This is a wonderful confirmation that our practice has become rooted in our bones. It is a part of our life forever. It may seem at this point that formal practice is no longer necessary. Nevertheless, we keep practicing. A sincere practitioner upholds their daily formal practice until the last breath leaves their lips. It is not at all an obligation, but a joy. Adepts place practice at the center of life and choose not to live a single day without it.

Direct Experience is the Best Teacher

Because of the simplicity of the Four Dignities, there is no risk of "doing it wrong." As long as you have self-honesty, it is possible to do this practice on your own, without a teacher. Sincerity and continuity are what matter most. Don't budge from what you are doing. For example, while practicing standing you may begin to feel itchy. Perhaps your lower back will ache a bit. During sitting, your foot may fall asleep. There will be many reasons to come out of the postures or be haphazard with your practice. Yet the power exists in staying the course; not with a sense of force, but with a spirit of giving yourself to the experience fully with less preference for a certain type of outcome. Within the discipline of holding to our posture and the routine of daily practice, wisdom begins to dawn. This is physical basis of self-honesty. Self-honesty is the guru. In other words, each situation is your perfect teacher.

Difficult emotions might come up. Blocked energies may start to unwind. And since we are not using a technique to make things happen in a yogic sense, there is no risk of doing it wrong. The power of the practice comes from holding firm to what you are doing, continuing regardless of what comes up. In an intense yoga pose, or vigorous breathing exercise, you have to use extreme caution not to push too far and injure yourself. There is a safety risk with highly technical practices. This is never that case with the Four Dignities. As long as you follow the axioms of Original Posture, Original Breath, and Original Nature, the practice is safe and self-regulating.

It's common that when people begin to practice the Four Dignities they become aware of places in the body where tension is held, asymmetries in the gait, mental neuroses, emotional difficulties. The practice is not producing these, but serving as a kind of gentle solvent that washes these out from hidden caverns. It's important to be kind to yourself when this happens. Maintaining an accepting and non-judgmental attitude is essential. At the same time, we must understand that the art of being kind also means continuing to practice even when it is challenging. It's like taking a load of laundry through all the cycles of the washer. The practice works deeply on body and mind. When we are thorough, an inner transformation begins to happen.

Chapter 11

QUESTIONS AND ANSWERS

"Leave it all behind you. Forget it. Go forth, unburdened with ideas and beliefs. Abandon all verbal structures, all relative truth, all tangible objectives. The Absolute can be reached by absolute devotion only. Don't be half-hearted."

Nisargadatta Maharaj

This section presents some of the most common questions asked by students over the years. Some of the questions and responses are listed verbatim from lecturers or correspondence with students; others are synthesized to represent the essence of a frequently asked question and my response.

Q: I am having a hard time understanding how the idea of intrinsic wholeness fits together with self-healing. Can you explain how these two relate in our practice?

A: Self-healing is a *function* of intrinsic wholeness. First, it is important to recognize the lack of any original flaw or problem. We have to work with the View. It is essential to debunk the learned notion that anything is missing. The doctrine of "original sin" is woven into many aspects of modern culture, especially our culture's ideas around medicine and healing. It can be tricky to see this because it is hiding in our assumptions. Self-healing starts by understanding that there is absolutely nothing wrong with you. Wholeness includes the inborn faculty of regeneration. It is not us or anyone else who does the healing. It is the Vital Force itself. Healing is a function of nature. It is operative within you all the time.

Q: What does it mean to be awake?

A: Awake means being without deception. Yet, strictly speaking, there is no such thing as awakening or being awake. There is only awakened action: playing the ball where it lands. Our natural and genuine response to things is awakened action, action-less action.

Q: Why do we do things 36 times during the closing sequence?

A: In most Asian spiritual traditions, the number 9 holds special significance. As the largest single-digit number, it represents completion: nine months in the womb, nine planets in our solar system. Therefore, multiples of nine are usually used for counting repetitions of exercises or mantras: 3 + 6 = 9. A traditional prayer mala has 108 beads, for example: 1 + 0 + 8 = 9. A full rotation finishes at 9, and then starts back at 1. This also reminds us that time is circular. We don't rush forward, since we only end up back where we stated. The number is not really that important, especially if it feels foreign for you. If you'd rather to do things 30 times, that is just as good.

Q: On the one hand, you say that the belly is our Center. On the other hand, you say that Being has no central location. This is confusing to me. Which is it, Center or no Center?

A: Dualistic mind is always looking for a clear one-sided answer. In linear dualistic thinking, as western academia most often teaches, the answer must be *this* or *that*. There is no room for two opposite truths to be simultaneously correct. We are taught that one answer must be wrong for the other to be right. Again, we have to look at our View. We have to admit that we are placing a demand on the situation that is philosophical, not actual. In reality, multiple meanings happen simultaneously. There is no problem with this. It is true that the belly is our physical Center of gravity. It is our Center of feeling and embodiment, how we were tethered to our mother *in utero*. Yet, at the same time, awareness and Vital Force have no central location. They are everywhere at the same time. Upon deepest investigation, no separate individual entity called a human being can be found; we can say that there is no abiding self. So, where is the center of an entity that exists only in relationship? There is no center. There is no periphery. Yet the absolute cannot be approached directly. Boundlessness cannot be apprehended. This is why we turn to the relative. The finite is the doorway into the infinite. Actually, they are one open space. It's a beautiful paradox. Relative and absolute truths are both valid. Here's the secret: breath, voice, and gravity are centered in the belly. The sense of "I" has its home here. Once this Center is felt, awareness and Vital Force naturally reveal their nature as without boundary or reference point. Our intellect will only grasp this to a certain degree. It is through practice and direct experience that realization crystallizes.

Q: What is the ideal way to schedule my practice times?

A: That really depends on your personal desire and schedule. More benefit comes from sustained moderate practice over time than with infrequent heroic efforts. Retreats and intensive practice periods are good if you can attend them, yet daily practice is the root. It has to be realistic for your lifestyle.

Q: During the practice of sitting, I feel an uncomfortable pressure in the front of my head. Why is that happening? Is it normal?

A: Pressure in the head is a sign of tension in the abdomen and too much mental effort toward concentrating. It is not "normal." However, it is quite common among meditation practitioners. Abdominal tension disturbs the diaphragm and changes the natural flow of blood and vital energy. It's a kind of reversal, where things go the opposite way. This can make the face feel hot and the head feel full. Over time, it can cause "meditation headaches" and digestive complications. The antidote is to relax physical and mental effort, and to allow Presence to drop from the head into the belly. You may have to do this over and over, as the habit of tensing the belly and placing Presence in the head is strong. Be patient and persistent.

Q: Can you say more about diet and meditation practice?

A: That is a big topic; we'd need the whole retreat to cover all the nuances. I'll say this: What you eat has a large impact on how your meditation goes. Meditation also helps you become more aware of how different foods make you feel. Diet is a very personal issue. I don't recommend any particular diet, other than one that is based in natural whole foods that are sustainably grown and raised without harmful chemicals. It is important to get to know your body and what types of food it thrives on. Whatever you can digest and assimilate is probably good for you. A particular diet plan might be great in theory, but if you don't digest the food well, it's not beneficial for you. Take care not to overeat. Eating more than your body requires, skipping meals when you are hungry, and eating erratically will certainly make meditation more difficult.

Q: There is a constant discomfort in my left ankle when I meditate. I am trying to let it go. I keep waiting for it to "self-resolve," as you say, but it doesn't go away.

A: We have spoken about your ankle. You told me everything that could be done medically has been done. So, as far as I understand, you have done your medical due diligence. Now you must bring your actual experience to your practice. Let's reflect on the View. "Trying to let it go" is a double mistake. First, trying to make anything specific happen during practice is not in harmony with the View. This comes from a subtle inner rejecting of your immediate situation. Consciousness is saying, "I don't like this. I want it to change, and I want it to change soon into something more to my liking." Reality does not work like that. We do not have such control. Second, "let it go" has a hidden assumption that "it," meaning the ankle pain, will go sooner than later. You actually *want* it to go. There is an inner pressure and tension behind the seemingly benign statement, "let it go." This is not the spirit of our practice. It reeks of hidden desire to have things go your way. This mistake is not unique to you. We are all guilty of it. None of us wants to suffer. We are all working with how to relate to the things that challenge us. But you have to remember that rejecting discomfort is one of the main causes of suffering. Replace trying with Being. And switch "let it go" with "release your hold." This means stop clutching to fixed ideas of how you think things could or should be. It is not a matter of what needs to be done, but what needs to be undone. It is sufficient to cease pushing and pulling on your experience. The natural law of change is always operative. Trust it. Each challenge contains its own resolution. If you can stop waiting for your ankle to self-resolve, it will probably resolve much more quickly.

Q: During seated meditation, my mouth fills up with so much saliva. Why does this happen?

A: As you relax, the body goes into a parasympathetic state. It starts balancing and repairing. Many people experience an increase in saliva production in the first year or two of meditation practice. It usually evens out with continued practice. Increased saliva flow is a sign of robust health. It's good for digestion and overall vitality. You may notice that you have more saliva throughout the day as well. However, during meditation, too much saliva means you'll be swallowing all the time. To mitigate this, place the tip of the tongue against the back of the teeth. Then allow the tongue to fill the mouth. Swallow. Maintain this position of the tongue while keeping the jaw and mouth soft and relaxed.

Q: I am so bad at meditation. My mind is always racing; it never stops. How long does it take to get good at this, to calm my mind?

A: We all go through this feeling at some point. The self-critic is a blabbermouth. Being "good" at meditation might be more of an obstacle than being "bad" at it. I never said the objective of meditation was to calm the mind or to stop the stream of thoughts. That is a popular misunderstanding about meditation. You are projecting this idea onto your practice. In the context of the Four Dignities, we practice meditation to have a complete experience of what we are. Don't try to attain any specific state. Don't try to be any different from how you are right now. Forget improvement. Forget ideas you've heard or read about stilling the mind. Forget accomplishments. Right now, you are just fine as you are. Don't kick up dust. Just practice!

Q: I've been practicing with you for a couple years, and just recently I have begun to feel an itchy crawly feeling on my shoulders during meditation. It feels like ants are crawling on me. What is causing this?

A: This feeling is quite common. It happens when the Vital Force starts to circulate more freely within the body. It's as if little rivers inside the body are opening up after a good rain. The body is healing itself. Relax and allow the process to run its course. It may happen for a while and then disappear.

Q: You mention the notion of the body as one hollow open space. The body is made of separate bones, muscles, and organs. How can it be a hollow space?

A: It is true, on the macro level, that the body is a bag of bones and blood. To the naked eye, the body is a physical thing. Yet, when we zoom in and observe more closely, we find that the body is actually made mostly of space. Even science has come to this understanding by looking at the construction of atoms and the behavior of subatomic particles. It's commonly understood that an atom is 99.9999999999999 percent space (yes, that's 13 nines after the decimal point). All tissues are made of cells, molecules, atoms, and subatomic particles. In essence, the body is energetically charged space. When we relax into any of the Four Dignities, we can experience this for ourselves. The whole body, as well as the entire universe, is a continuous field of luminous space. Obstructions are conceptual only. During our practice, awareness permeates this singular body from head to toe, and from skin to bone. To make the idea of limitless space tangible for the mind to grasp, we say that the belly is the Center of our experience.

Q: Can you summarize the idea of dignity again and explain how it relates to our practice?

A: Dignity stems from the whole person. It is an inborn trait of human beings. It is not the result of social status or class. Our practice is to express dignity as part of our essential humanness while we walk, stand, sit, and lie down. In other words, all the time. Dignity is upheld by being genuine and human-hearted in all our endeavors.

Q: Other practices I've done give a specific object to focus on, such as a mantra, deity, or specific energy center. What is the object of our meditation?

A: The object of our meditation is life as it is. Posture creates the platform for breathing. Breathing animates the flesh of posture. In both cases, naturalness is the Way. The object of daily practice is to return to spontaneity and express genuine humanity. Sincerity and consistency are what matter most, not specific objects or intensity of concentration. The point is to be as you are. You can't make an object out of what you are; then which one would be you, the subject or the object? Continue reflecting on the View until this becomes clear. Then, check your understanding against your direct experience through practice. This is the direct Path.

Q: I was always taught to have clear goals and to pursue them passionately to get true results. Now you are telling me that to get Fruition in this practice I have to let go of having a goal. How can I benefit from spiritual practice if I don't have a clear goal to achieve?

A: The presumption of a specific goal in mind, with certain benefits to reap later, is contradictory to the View of natural perfection. Chasing enlightenment, transcendence, Samadhi, bliss: this is consumerism at its best. Every goal begets another desire to satisfy. There is no end to the anxiety cycle. It is based in the assumption that something is fundamentally missing from your experience. Religion and advertising taught you this. You became the consumer they have been molding since childhood. Break the mold! It probably never occurred to you to make a goal of being a woman. It would be ridiculous. Since you already are a woman, the notion of needing to gain such a quality does not arise. The same goes for spiritual fulfillment. You already have it, but fail to recognize the fact. You have been whole from the beginning. Not a single thing is lacking. You are perfect as you are. I see the obvious in you; I'm sure your mother does too, yet you doubt it. This is a learned habit. Now, do you see the absurdity of spiritual goal setting? If you still have to use the goal–reward model, then do it like this: Make it your goal to see through the base assumptions of your own point of view. Make it your goal to investigate your beliefs and the stories you weave to support them. Right before you go chasing a goal, ask yourself these questions: What is the source of my discontentment? What am I trying to get over *there* that I don't have right *here*? What am I running from?

Q: In Buddhism, the idea of "right mindfulness" is an important aspect of dharma practice. How would you explain this in terms of the Four Dignities?

A: Great question. "Right mindfulness" means non-preferential awareness. It means pure awareness, without goal seeking. I usually don't use the term "right mindfulness" because I think westerners often misinterpret mindfulness as a purely mental quality. Proper practice of the Four Dignities depends on an integration of body, mind, and breath. Our practice is to cultivate immediate Presence and genuine humanity. It is a full-being endeavor, not just mental. Think about the posture and attentiveness you would assume if you were selected to present a gift of honor to the Dalai Lama or the Queen of England. You would do your very best to embody virtue, dignity and wholesomeness, wouldn't you? This scenario evokes the idea of appropriate posture, breath, and Presence. This is "right mindfulness."

Q: I suffer from severe anxiety. After practicing meditation for a while, I have come to realize that I am afraid of facing myself. I fear that if I practice the Four Dignities sincerely, my anxiety will get worse. There is this great darkness; I am worried that I may be consumed by my inner demons.

A: Thank you for sharing this; it takes courage. Your vulnerability empowers us all. Keep in mind that it's not only you who struggles with this. You are already practicing the Four Dignities. The insight you had in regard to facing yourself shows that self-honesty is operative. Your experience of anxiety might get a little more intense as you stop running from your feelings. It may get a little messy, but that's the cost of becoming real. The only danger is in continuing to avoid yourself. All anxiety has its roots in self-centeredness. We are concerned with our entertainment, our health, our possessions, our beliefs. We desperately want comfort and security. Yet, in nature, there is none. Nothing is secure. Everything is changing too fast to be secure. This scares us. To be free of anxiety and fear, you have to see things as they actually are. You have to fully embrace your personal situation. Stop resisting your own experience. Embrace it and let it be. It's important to keep studying the View until you fully understand the cosmology of insufficiency and the truth of intrinsic wholeness. Once you see through the fallacy of original sin, and understand that indeed all is well, anxiety will be a distant memory. What does your life look like if nothing is missing and your experience is actually complete of-itself? Face yourself with open-heartedness and watch demons turn to flowers.

Q: What is the relationship between Fruition and karma?

A: Fruition is not realized as a result of your actions. Don't look for it as an effect of what you do. This is self-cherishing. Fruition has nothing to do with your personal efforts. Yet, if you do not practice, there is no Fruition. Fruition is so-of-itself. It is action-less action. It is outside the cycle of cause and effect. Fruition is the basic ground; it is the way-things-are. Practice is the unabashed expression of suchness. Again, keep studying the View and understand the true meaning of View, Method, and Fruition.

Q: As a long-time yoga teacher, I have seen many people get "burnt out" by their practice. They become ungrounded, hypersensitive, can't digest food well, etc. I've seen it happen with women especially. What causes this?

A: Too much effort disperses our vital energy, alters our endocrine system, and causes premature aging. I have seen this happen with people who are overly ambitious in their practice of Hatha or Kundalini Yoga. Stoking the fire too aggressively burns up the life-essence (Chinese *jing*, Sanskrit *ojas*). Excess fire is especially problematic for women. We have to learn to relax into our practice, to reduce effort. *Yin* and *yang* come into balance when we stop pushing.

Q: Can you explain Exposure, Contemplation, and Embodiment in another way so I can understand these better?

A: Hearing, study, and practice. Hearing is a transmission. Study is how we confront our self-deception. Practice is a creative act; it's how we express our nature.

Q: I understand we don't practice to attain anything. So why practice at all?

A: We practice because we have a tendency to do things. We practice because we can't stop walking, standing, sitting, and lying down. Just try to stop doing any one of these, and you will understand. Try to only stand or sit or lie down. In fact, lying down is the easiest. Try to lie down for as long as you can. At some point you will have to get up. Notice what happens the moment before you actually get up. What is it that moves you from your position? Things move and change. Practice is nothing more than moving and changing. That's why we practice.

Q: I understand the notion of non-abiding, but what makes the appearance of a separate and abiding self seem so real?

A: The appearance of an abiding self shows up in the tension between what-is and our preferences, how we want things to be. Disdain for pain produces the experience of a solid "me." Excessive craving for pleasure produces the experience of a solid "me." Caught in the tension of craving and aversion, the "I" seems very solid and real. However, in the openness of pure being, this knot is found to be nothing but a mirage. We can't say "there is no self," we can't say "there is a self." Both of these make a *thing* out of no-thing. This is why we point to direct experience. Direct experience is immediate and fleeting. It happens; but to whom? Of this, we are not certain. Uncertainty is the best place to find your answer.

Q: If Fruition is not an accomplishment, what is it?

A: You have already accomplished so many things. Where have all these accomplishment gotten you? There is a basic assumption that accomplishments are ends in themselves. If this were the case, you'd already be finished, satisfied. All accomplishments dissolve into the current of change; anything you gain will also be lost. No accomplishment is final. Therefore, we understand that Fruition is not an accomplishment. It is Original Nature. It is not an accomplishment for water to be wet. It might be better to think of Fruition as that which is always present. It is behind the need to chase success. Practice every day for a few years. Keep checking your View. Things will become clear through your direct experience, not theoretical understanding.

Q: What does it mean to take refuge?

A: It means different things in different traditions. Ultimately, outside of lineage and specific tradition, taking refuge means abiding in suchness. It means you have seen the way things are, and, in the silence of your own heart, have given up the habit of wishing reality were different. It means you have surrendered to what-is.

Q: What do you think about yoga, qigong, and other esoteric energy practices in relationship to meditation?

A: They are wonderful—made for each other. However, it is only in the right frame of mind (View) that yogic practices take on any profound significance. Without proper understanding of View, yogic techniques are likely to compound the predicament of tension and falsehood. First, we have to correct our View. We have to work with our frame of mind, if we are to use mind-body practices with any effectiveness whatsoever.

Q: I understand the principle of intrinsic wholeness. Intellectually, I see there is no need to strive to attain anything from my meditation practice. But, if I'm totally honest with myself, I am still striving for something. There is this unrest. There is this wanting inside me. I keep acting in a way that I know to be untrue. It feels like torture. How do I resolve this?

A: Sounds as if your conduct is not representative of your true heart. You are aware that you are acting contrary to your nature. Find out why. The next time it is about to happen, slow down and observe. Find out what type of feelings and thoughts precede the habit of causing your own unrest.

Q: What is the meaning of initiation? Some teachers say that you must receive initiation for spiritual practice to be effective.

A: Initiation happens the moment you stop running from yourself. It is between you and the universe. It's not about getting a new name in a foreign language or receiving fancy silk vestments for a special ceremony. It's about honesty. It's the moment you admit to yourself that all your little addictions are poor attempts at trying to avoid the discomfort and claustrophobia of being *you*. A teacher may point out your habit of self-deceit, or you can admit it to yourself. Either way, self-honesty is the precursor to initiation.

Q: You talk about the idea of stillness in motion, and movement in stillness. I don't think I understand exactly what this means. Could you explain?

A: Stillness and movement are relative. For example, in sitting meditation we keep the body relatively still. This means we don't intentionally move the limbs or adjust our posture once we're settled. However, inside this stillness, there are many layers of movement. The diaphragm is moving up and down. The breath is moving in and out. The heart is pumping. The blood is moving through the vessels. The idea is to allow the inborn rhythms of movement to happen naturally by releasing tension and softening within. On the other hand, during movement we notice a sense of stillness within. It is through the open quality of pure awareness that we have this sense. In walking, for example, we have the feeling of stillness in motion. The body moves, but there is something still about the whole dynamic. Movement and stillness, like emptiness and form, always arise together.

ENDNOTES

1.   See Komjathy, *Redoubled Yang's Fifteen Discourses to Establish the Teachings*, which is part of the early Complete Reality School textual collection, considered one of the most clear and direct manuals on Daoist Complete Reality practice.

2.   A comprehensive 600-verse pre-Mahayana treatise compiled by Vasubandhu, circa 380 CE.

3.   Ma Yu (1123–1183), one of the seven masters, called "the Seven Real Men" of the Quanzhen ("Complete Reality") School of Daoism.

4.   Fukuoka, *One Straw Revolution*.

5.   Bhikkhu, *Small Boat, Great Mountain*, 72.

6.   The second-most influential text of Daoism, after the *Dao De Jing*, espousing the philosophy of spontaneity and the path to personal freedom through self-cultivation. Like the *Dao De Jing*, the *Zhaungzi* is grounded in the ideas of Dao ("way") and De ("virtue").

7.   Komjathy, *Scripture for Daily Internal Practice*, 8.

8.   Qiu Chuji (1148–1227), founder of the Long Men ("Dragon Gate") sect of Daoism.

9.   Thank you, Liu Ming, for the poignant reminder.

10. http://ds9.ssl.berkeley.edu/solarweek/DISCUSSION/howold.html

11. The *Heart Sutra* expresses Mahayana Buddhism in 14 Sanskrit *slokas* (206 Chinese characters, 16 English sentences). With laser-like accuracy and clarity, this short text describes the direct path to awakening as *Prajnaparmita* ("Perfection of Wisdom"), seeing things as-they-are.

12. Conferring of spiritual "energy" from one person to another.

13. In the Ancient Chinese traditions that inform medicine, martial arts and meditation, the central channel is called *Chong Mai* ("Penetrating Meridian"). In the ancient Indian systems, informing Ayurveda, yoga and Tantra, the central channel is called *Sushumna Nadi* ("Middle River").

14. The inherent capacity of body and mind to adapt and flourish regardless of the circumstances.

15. Chinese *sanbao*. The Three Treasures are *jing* ("essence"), *qi* ("energy"), and *shen* ("spirit").

16. *Dantien* is a Chinese term literally meaning "elixir field" or "field of potential." There are three main *dantien* in the body: lower belly, chest, and head. In this case my teacher was referring to walking from the lower *dantien*, the belly.

17. A hot-excessive type constitution or condition is characterized by red lips and flushed face, frequent sweating, irritability and bursts of anger, burning eyes, skin rashes or acne, and intolerance to heat and humidity.

18. A cold-deficient type constitution or condition is characterized by low energy, cold hands and feet, intolerance to cold, wind, and loud noises, and a tendency to be overly sensitive or susceptible.

19. Chinese medical classic from the second century BCE.

BIBLIOGRAPHY

Akers, Brian Dana, trans. *The Hatha Yoga Pradipika*. Woodstock, NY: Yoga Vidya, 2002.

An, Liu. *The Huainanzi*. New York, NY: Columbia University Press, 2010.

Barks, Coleman and Green, Michael. *The Illuminated Rumi*. New York, NY: Broadway Books, 1997.

Bhikkhu, Amaro. *Small Boat, Great Mountain*. Redwood Valley, CA: Abhayagiri Buddhist Monastery, 2003.

Bhikkhu, Thanissaro, trans. *Cankama Sutta: Walking (AN 5.29)*. Available at www.accessto insight.org/tipitaka/an/an05/an05.029.than.html, accessed on February 16, 2012.

Byron, Thomas, trans. *The Heart of Awareness: A Translation of the Ashtavakra Gita*. Boston, MA: Shambhala Publications, 1990.

Chuen, Master Lam Kam. *The Way of Energy: Mastering the Chinese Art of Internal Strength with Chi Kung Exercise*. London: Gaia Books, 1991.

Den Dekker, Peter. *The Dynamics of Standing Still*. Haarlem, Netherlands: Back2Base Publishing, 2010.

Dowman, Keith. *Natural Perfection: Longchenpa's Radical Dzogchen*. Somerville, MA: Wisdom Publications, 2010.

Dürckheim, Karlfried Graf. *Hara: The Vital Center of Man*. Rochester, VT: Inner Traditions, 2004.

Feng, Gia-Fu, trans. and English, Jane, trans. *Lau Tzu: Tao Te Ching*. New York, NY: Vintage Books, 1972.

Fukuoka, Masanobu. *One Straw Revolution*. New York, NY: New York Review of Books, 2009.

Godman, David, ed. *Be As You Are: The Teachings of Sri Ramana Maharshi*. New Delhi: Penguin Books India, 1985.

Hanh, Thich Nhat. *The Long Road Turns to Joy*. Berkeley, CA: Parallax Press, 1996.

Hartranft, Chip, trans. *The Yoga-Sutra of Patanjali*. Boston, MA: Shambhala Publications, 2003.

Iyengar, B.K.S. *Light on Yoga*. New York, NY: Schocken Books, 1979.

Johnson, Will. *The Posture of Meditation*. Boston, MA: Shambhala Publications, 1996.

Johnson, Will. *Breathing Through the Whole Body*. Rochester, VT: Inner Traditions, 2012.

Jotika, U. and Dhamminda, U. trans. *Mahasatipatthana Sutta*. Maymyo, Burma: Migadavun Monastery, 1986.

Khyentse, Dilgo. *The Heart of Compassion: The Thirty-Seven Verses on the Practice of a Bodhisattva*. Boston, MA: Shambhala Publications, 2007.

Kohn, Livia. *Meditation Works: In the Hindu, Buddhist, and Daoist Traditions*. Magdalena, NM: Three Pines Press, 2008.

Komjathy, Louis, trans. *Book of Venerable Masters*. Hong Kong: Yuen Yuen Institute, 2008.

Komjathy, Louis, trans. *Inward training*. Hong Kong: Yuen Yuen Institute, 2008.

Komjathy, Louis, trans. *Redoubled Yang's Fifteen Discourses*. Hong Kong: Yuen Yuen Institute, 2008.

Komjathy, Louis, trans. *Scripture for Daily Internal Practice*. Hong Kong: Yuen Yuen Institute, 2008.

Lau, D.C. and Ames, Roger T. *Yuan Dao: Tracing Dao to its Source*. New York, NY: Random House, 1998.

Liu, Da. *Taoist Health Exercise Book*. New York, NY: Links Books, 1974.

Longchenpa. *You Are the Eyes of the World*. Translated by Kennard Lipman and Merrill Peterson. Ithaca, NY: Snow Lion Publications, 2000.

Maharaj, Sri Nisargadatta. *I Am That*. Durham, NC: Acorn Press, 1982.

Mallinson, James, trans. *The Shiva Samhita*. Woodstock, NY: Yoga Vidya, 2007.

Ming, Liu. *The Way of the Three Treasures*. Oakland, CA: Da Yuan Circle, 2008.

Mitchell, Stephen. *Tao Te Ching*. New York, NY: Harper Perennial, 1992.

Nyanadhammo, Venerable Ajan. *Walking Meditation*. Ubon Rachathani, Thailand: The Sangha of Wat Pah Nanachat, 2003.

Pine, Red, trans. *The Zen Teachings of Bodhidharma*. New York, NY: North Point Press, 1987.

Ramacharaka, Yogi. *The Hindu-Yogi: Science of Breath*. Yogi Publication Society, 1932.

Reynolds, John Myrdhin, trans. *Self-Liberation through Seeing with Naked Awareness*. Barrytown, NY: Station Press, 1989.

Sheng-Yen, Chan Master. *There is No Suffering*. Elmhurst, NY: Dharma Drum, 2001.

Suzuki Roshi, Shunryu. *Zen Mind, Beginner's Mind*. New York, NY: Weatherhill, 1999.

Tanahashi, Kazuaki, ed. *Moon in a Dewdrop: Writing of Zen Master Dogen*. New York, NY: North Point Press, 1985.

Trungpa, Chögyam and Gimian, Carolyn Rose, eds. *Smile at Fear: Awakening the True Heart of Bravery*. Boston, MA: Shambhala Publications, 2009.

Trungpa, Chögyam and Lief, Judith L., eds. *The Path of Individual Liberation*. Boston, MA: Shambhala Publications, 2013.

Van Lysebeth, Andre. *Pranayama: The Yoga of Breathing*. London: Unwin Hyman, 1979.

Wang, Xuanjie and Moffett, J.P.C. *Traditional Chinese Therapeutic Exercises: Standing Pole*. Beijing, China: Foreign Language Press, 1994.

Wilberg, Peter. *The Little Book of Hara*. Amazon Digital Service: Kindle Edition, 2011.

Wilson, William Scott. *The One Taste of Truth: Zen and the Art of Drinking Tea*. Boston, MA: Shambhala Publications, 2012.

Wu, Zhongxian. *Vital Breath of the Dao: Chinese Shamanic Tiger Qigong*. St. Paul, MN: Dragon Door Publications, 2006.

Yogendra, Shri. *Yoga Personal Hygiene*. Bombay: Yoga Institute, 1931.

INDEX

INDEX

qi
  creative force of the divine
    83
  and fetal positions 160
  and gravity 61
  Hao Datong's quote 16
  "Sink the qi, lift the spirit"
    (Chinese saying) 100
  and spiritual escapism 37
  and standing 99, 102, 104,
    107
"qi washing" 173–5
qigong 81, 100, 173, 210
Qing Jing 11–12
Qiu, Chuji 19
Quarter Lotus 126, 131–2,
  131
questions and answers
  abiding self 208–9
  ankle pain and "release your
    hold" vs "let it go"
    201–2
  anxiety and facing oneself
    206–7
  awakeness 198
  body as one hollow space
    203–4
  "burnt out" by practice
    207–8
  Center of Being and Vital
    Force 199–200
  closing sequence, number 9
    and 36 times 198–9
  diet and meditation 200–1
  dignity 204
  exposure, contemplation
    and embodiment,
    synonyms for 208
  Fruition and karma 207
  Fruition vs
    accomplishments 209
  goal setting 205–6
  initiation 210–11
  intrinsic wholeness and
    self-healing 198
  intrinsic wholeness and
    striving compulsion
    210
  meditation and itchy
    feeling in shoulders
    203
  meditation and racing
    minds 202–3
  meditation and yoga or
    qigong 210
  meditation, object of 204–5

practice times 200
reasons for practicing 208
right mindfulness 206
sitting and pressure in the
  head 200
sitting and saliva
  production 202
stillness and motion/
  movement 211
taking refuge 209–10

Ramana, Maharshi 17, 114
reclining practice *see* lying
  down
reflection 16, 20
  see also self-reflection
refuge *see* taking refuge
relaxation
  and enjoyment 71
  and tension 44–5, 69
religion
  and doubt 186, 187
  and ego-grasping 70
  and goal setting 205
  and law of change 29
  and meditation 12
  see also original sin concept
right mindfulness 206
  see also awareness
Root Sequence 166–7, 172
rooting, and standing 99–100
rub (the skin) 173–5
Rumi 77

saliva
  sitting and saliva
    production 202
  swallowing of 173, 175
  swishing of 173, 175
Samadhi 184, 205
Savasana (Corpse Pose)
  147–8, 157
sayings
  on breathing (Chinese) 64
  "Don't kick up the dust"
    71, 203
  "Keep the head cool and
    the belly warm" 54
  "Only don't know" (Zen)
    184
  "The secret is behind the
    paper door" (Daoist)
    66
  "Sink the qi, lift the spirit"
    (Chinese) 100

  on tension and relaxation
    (Chinese) 69
  on walk/stand/sit/lie down
    (Daoist) 75
  "What you resist persists"
    100
science
  and concept of space 203–4
  and doubt 186
  and ego-grasping 70
  and gravity 60
  and law of change 29
seating *see* sitting
"secret is behind the paper
  door" (Daoist saying) 66
seeking 69–71
Seiza (Floor-Kneeling) 117,
  138–40, *138*
self *see* abiding self; ego; "I
  don't know"
self-aggrandizement 36–7
self-cultivation
  art of 10
  Chinese systems 173
  and dignity 14
  and discipline 183
  and meditation 12
  and Original Breath 66
  and *tathatā* ("suchness" or
    "thusness") 15
  and tension vs relaxation 44
self-doubt 187
  see also doubt, paradox of
self-hatred 36–7
self-healing 191–3, 198
self-honesty 36–7, 38, 188,
  194–5, 206–7, 211
self-reflection 15, 37, 53
  from contemplation to
    embodiment 38–9
  from exposure to
    contemplation 22–3
  see also reflection
sequences 166–8, 172
  closing sequence 173–6,
    198–9
sexual energy, and Burmese
  Position 130
Shakti (primal energy) 123–4
shaktipat 37
shi gi ("four bodily presences/
  noble rites") 11
shins, and standing 102
Shiva Samhita 174
shoes 170
  see also feet

[221]

Zhuangzi

ABOUT THE AUTHOR

Cain Carroll is a pioneering teacher, speaker, and author in the field of self-healing and embodied spirituality. He has studied the martial, healing, and spiritual arts of Asia since childhood. Cain is founder of the Taoflow Yoga system, co-author of *Partner Yoga: Making Contact for Physical, Emotional and Spiritual Growth, Mudras of India*, and *Mudras of Yoga Card Deck*, and creator of three instructional DVDs: *Pain-Free Joints, Heal Neck & Shoulder Pain*, and *Digestive Power*. Visit www.caincarroll.com.